EL GHALIA
Magazine

THAILAND

Welcome to Thailand!

Are you looking for a holiday without the burden of heavy luggage? Thailand is the place to go. With its cheap flights and restaurants full of delicious food, it's easy to see why people keep returning. Whether you want an adventure in Bangkok or a relaxing beach getaway in Phuket, we have the perfect trip at hand!

If you're visiting Thailand for the first time or the second time, our comprehensive, WELL-DESIGNED guidebook has everything you need to enjoy your stay. From must-see attractions and historical backgrounds to a list of activities and getting around tips, this guide has it all. With detailed maps and a wealth of information, our guidebook will make your visit to Thailand unforgettable!

Travel Plan :

Kanchanaburi

Khao Yai National Park

★ Bangkok

Pattaya

Ko Chang

Khao Sok
National Park

Krabi
Province

Phuket

⬤ : Cities

⬤ : Optional Destinations

⬤ : Major Destinations

List of Content

Bar color - Bangkok

Thailand's bustling, frenetic capital, known among the Thai as Krung Thep

Bar color - Khao Sok National Park

One of the most beautiful wildlife reserves in Thailand

Bar color - Phuket

The original Thai paradise island, now very developed but with some still beautiful beaches

Bar color - Krabi Province

Beach and water sports mecca in the south, includes Ao Nang, Rai Leh, Ko Phi Phi, and Ko Lanta

Bangkok

Thailand's bustling, frenetic capital, known among the Thai as Krung Thep

Bangkok, Thailand

Overview

Bangkok (Thai: กรุงเทพฯ Krung Thep) is the capital and largest city of Thailand. With a population of over eleven million inhabitants, Bangkok is by far Thailand's main city. Its high-rise buildings, heavy traffic congestion, intense heat and naughty nightlife do not immediately give you a warm welcome — but don't let your first impression mislead you. It is one of Asia's most cosmopolitan cities with magnificent palaces, authentic canals, busy markets and a vibrant nightlife that has something for everyone.

For years, it was only a small trading post at the banks of the Chao Phraya River, until King Rama I, the first monarch of the present Chakri dynasty, turned it into the capital of Siam in 1782, after the burning of Ayutthaya by Burmese invaders. Since then, Bangkok has turned into a national treasure house and functions as Thailand's spiritual, cultural, political, commercial, educational and diplomatic centre.

Districts

Bangkok is a huge and modern city humming with nightlife and fervor. Administratively, it is split up into 50 districts (เขต khet), which are further split into 180 sub-districts (แขวง khwaeng), but these are more often used in official business and for addresses. Visitors will find the conceptual division below of the main areas more useful for getting around.

● Siam Square

The area around Siam Square, including Ratchaprasong and Phloen Chit Road, is Bangkok's modern commercial core, full of glitzy malls and hotels. The Skytrain intersection at Siam Square is the closest thing Bangkok has to a centre.

● Sukhumvit

The long Sukhumvit Road is an exclusive district popular among expatriates and upper class locals. It is filled with quality hotels, restaurants and nightclubs. Part of its nightlife represents Bangkok's naughty image, particularly Soi Cowboy and Nana Entertainment Plaza.

● Silom

The area around Silom Road and Sathorn Road is Thailand's sober financial centre by day, but Bangkok's primary party district by night when quarters like the infamous Patpong come alive.

Districts

- **Rattanakosin**
Between the river and Sukhumvit lies the densely packed "Old Bangkok", home to Bangkok's best-known sights, such as the Grand Palace and Wat Pho

- **Khao San Road**
On the northern part of Rattanakosin, Bangkok's backpacker mecca Khao San Road and the surrounding district of Banglamphu have everything a budget traveller could possibly be looking for.

- **Yaowarat and Phahurat**
Along Yaowarat Road you will find Bangkok's Chinatown, while Phahurat Road is the home of the city's sizeable Indian community. This multicultural district is filled with seafood restaurants and street markets.

- **Dusit**
This leafy, European-style area is the political centre of Thailand, home to numerous political institutions and the monarchy. Its breezy palaces, lush gardens and broad avenues give this district its distinct character.

- **Thonburi**
The quieter west bank of the Chao Phraya River. Most visitors explore this district with a canal tour, at least taking in Wat Arun, the Royal Barges National Museum and one of the floating markets.

Districts

- **Pratunam**

Pratunam is a large garment market with hundreds of fashion stores selling both retail and wholesale. It also includes Baiyoke Tower II and Victory Monument.

- **Phahonyothin**

The area around Phahonyothin Road and Viphavadi Rangsit Road is a large suburb in northern Bangkok. In weekends, it is the best place to go hunting for bargains. The Chatuchak Weekend Market has more than 8,000 stalls selling anything and everything under the sun.

- **Ratchadaphisek**

Since the completion of the metro line, Ratchadaphisek Road has developed into an entertainment mecca for the locals. The sois, (side streets off busy main roads of "Ratchada" are popular clubbing spots, as is Royal City Avenue (RCA).

- **Ramkhamhaeng**

Along Ramkhamhaeng Road lies a vast residential area with big shopping malls and amusement parks (like Safari World). Each neighbourhood has its own distinct character, but Hua Mak and Bang Kapi stand out as lively areas with many students from the universities.

Bangkok Map

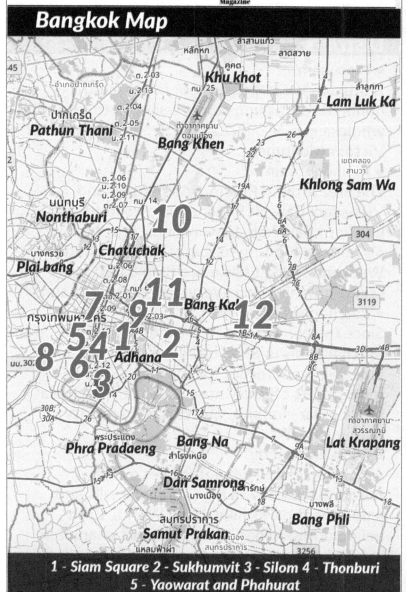

1 - Siam Square 2 - Sukhumvit 3 - Silom 4 - Thonburi
5 - Yaowarat and Phahurat
6 - Rattanakosin 7 - Pratunam 8 - Khao San Road
9 - Dusit 10 - Phahonyothin 11 - Ratchadaphisek
12 - Ramkhamhaeng

EL GHALIA
Magazine

Learn more

Just under 14 degrees north of the equator, Bangkok is a tropical metropolis that is also one of the most traveller-friendly cities in Asia. A furious assault on the senses, visitors are immediately confronted by the heat, the pollution, unpleasant smells, and the irrepressible smile worn by many Thais. Despite the sensationalised international news reports and first impressions, the city is surprisingly safe (except for petty crimes) and more organised than it initially appears, and is full of hidden gems waiting to be discovered. The high relative humidity and warm temperature favour the growth of tropical plants — you'll find exotic orchids and delicious fruit everywhere. Bougainvillea and frangipani bloom practically all over the city. Thai cuisine is justifiably famous, varied, and affordable. Bangkok for many represents the quintessential Asian capital. Saffron-robed monks, garish neon signs, graceful Thai architecture, spicy dishes, colourful markets, traffic jams, and the tropical climate come together in a happy coincidence. It is difficult to leave with only lukewarm impressions of the city.

Learn more

History

"Bangkok" was originally a small village on the west bank of the Chao Phraya River. After the fall of Ayutthaya in the late 18th century, King Taksin the Great turned that village into Siam's new capital and renamed it Thonburi. In 1782, King Rama I moved the capital to the eastern bank of the river at Rattanakosin; originally the site of a Chinese community, which was moved outside of the new city walls to Yaowarat. King Rama I named the city Krung Thep, as it is now known to Thais and which in English translates as the "City of Angels".

The full name "Krungthepmahanakhon Amonrattanakosin Mahintharayutthaya Mahadilokphop Noppharatratchathaniburirom Udomratchaniwetmahasathan Amonphimanawatansathit Sakkathattiyawitsanukamprasit" (กรุงเทพมหานคร อมรรัตนโกสินทร์ มหินทรายุธยามหาดิลกภพ นพรัตน์ราชธานี บุรีรมย์อุดมราชนิเวศน์มหาสถาน อมรพิมานอวตารสถิต สักกะทัตติยะวิษณุกรรมประสิทธิ์) is listed as the world's longest location name by the Guinness Book of Records; an English rendering goes like this: "The city of angels, the great city.

Bangkok, Thailand

Learn more

History

The residence of the Emerald Buddha, the impregnable city of Ayutthaya of God Indra, the grand capital of the world endowed with nine precious gems, the happy city, abounding in an enormous Royal Palace that resembles the heavenly abode where reigns the reincarnated god, a city given by Indra and built by Vishnukarn". Foreigners never caught on to the change, so in foreign languages Krung Thep inherited the name Bangkok, which became its formal English name. For Thais, the name Bangkok refers to the former village on the west bank of the Chao Phraya, which was incorporated into Greater Bangkok in 1971.

Climate

According to the World Meteorological Organization, Bangkok is the world's hottest city. Just 14 degrees north of the equator, Bangkok is sunny at all times of the year with temperatures over 30°C (86°F).

The most pleasant time to visit is the cool season that lasts from Nov-Feb. It is both the coolest and driest period — the Emerald Buddha statue in Wat Phra Kaeo even wears a scarf during this period! Don't think that's necessary though — daytime temperatures still hover around 30°C (86°F), but it does cool down into the lower 20s as it gets dark (lower 70s in Fahrenheit), and on rare occasions can even dip as low as 15°C.

Learn more

Climate

March and April represent the hot season, and hot it is — 35°C (95°F) on average, but don't be surprised to see heat indices rising into the 50s °C (around 120 °F+). This is the worst season to visit Bangkok, so plan in a lot of air-conditioned shopping mall visits and get a hotel with a swimming pool. Then there's the wet season that runs from May-Oct. Expect massive downpours resulting in floods all over the city, and spells of thunder at times. It's not all bad though — the afternoon showers are actually a pleasant way to cool down from the heat, and while they may last all day, usually they're over within an hour. Extreme rainfall happens in September and October, so these months are best avoided. Whatever season you're visiting, don't take the weather lightly — temple-tramping in the scorching afternoon sun can be a challenge, so come well-prepared. Dress lightly for the weather, but keep in mind that some palaces and temples (notably the Grand Palace) have a strict dress code, i.e., everyone must fully cover their torso, legs and upper arms. So shorts, halter tops, etc. will deny you entry. At entrances to some major attractions, vendors may rent needed coverage.

Getting In

By plane

Suvarnabhumi Airport

● Suvarnabhumi Airport (สุวรรณภูมิ BKK IATA) (30 km (19 mi) east of Bangkok). Space-age Suvarnabhumi Airport started operations in Sep 2006 and is now Bangkok's main airport and one of the busiest airports in Southeast Asia. It is used for international and domestic flights to Bangkok. There is only one terminal building, which covers both domestic and international flights. It is huge, and by some measures the world's largest, so allow time for getting around. There are two immigration sections, but processing time can be lengthy, at least 30 min and on bad days almost 2 hr.

On the basement level of the passenger terminal, the Airport Rail Link offers a speedy train service to downtown. It's also a way of avoiding Bangkok's horrendous rush hour traffic, particularly when it's raining. Trains depart 06:00-midnight every day. The City Line is a commuter rail line that stops at all stations. Trains leave every 10-13 min, and after Makkasan station they continue to Ratchaprarop and Phaya Thai stations. The ride to Phaya Thai takes 26 min from the airport and costs 45 baht.

Getting In

By plane

You can also take a free shuttle bus to the airport bus terminal aka Transportation Centre to catch inexpensive city buses. These may be convenient if you are going to a suburban area like Rangsit or Bang Kapi. Since June 2017 express bus S1 runs from the terminal building to Khao San Road.

If you need a taxi, ordinary metered taxis are available on the first floor (one floor below arrivals). Follow the "public taxi" signs that lead to the official taxi queue outside of the airport premises. Avoid the touts in the arrival hall; the taxis they are trying to get you into are mostly likely illegal, and the risk of getting ripped off is much higher with them. ATM-style ticket booths dispense numbered slips, with the number indicating the bay in which your taxi is parked. You can choose between a normal taxi good for 2 adults with baggage and a big taxi. Keep the slip since it helps to make a complaint if the driver scams you. There is a surcharge on top of the meter (not per passenger), meaning that trips to the city will cost 250-400 baht plus possible expressway tolls of 50 and 25 baht (March 2020) depending on route. Make sure you have change ready to pass to the toll operators to avoid being overcharged for the tolls later on. The ride takes about 45–60 min depending on traffic and destination.

Getting In

By plane

● **Don Mueang Airport**

Don Mueang Airport (ดอนเมือง DMK IATA) (about 30 km (19 mi) north of Sukhumvit). This was Bangkok's main airport until 2006. These days, the airport primarily caters to budget carriers, and handles flights by Thai Lion Air, Scoot, Nok Air, Orient Thai and Air Asia. It is a bit harder to reach DMK than BKK due to the absence of a practical rail connection.

Taxi : the public taxi stand is on the end of the arrival area. Follow the signs to the taxi stand. (Don't be fooled by all the taxi service booths in the main hall.) The same booth and slip system as at Suvarnabhumi Airport is used here. If the queue at the taxi stand is long or you need a more spacious car, you may want to book a (so-called) limousine taxi from the desks in the terminal. This will get you a slightly nicer car at about twice the price. There is also an unofficial taxi queue (but for proper metered taxis) on the main road right outside the terminal, to get there, use the bridge towards the railway station, but get off down the narrow staircase before crossing the main road (using this queue can cut the wait considerably and avoid the airport surcharge). Ignore any touts outside and do not get into any car with white licence plates.

Getting In

By bus

When buying tickets for buses out of Bangkok, it's best to skip travel agents and their private buses, and get the tickets for public buses directly at Bangkok's three public bus terminals. These buses are cheaper, safer, faster, more comfortable and won't scam you onto a clapped-out minibus halfway along the way or to a bedbug-infested hotel at the end. Each of these long haul bus terminals serve a different direction. They are purposefully located in off-central locations, so the long-haul buses avoid the heavy traffic congestion in the centre of the city. They are :

● Eastern Bus Terminal (Ekkamai (เอกมัย)), ☎ +66 2 391-2504. A relatively compact terminal right next to Ekkamai BTS station in Sukhumvit. Ekkamai serves destinations in Eastern Thailand, including Pattaya, Rayong, Ban Phe (for Ko Samet), Chanthaburi and Trat. If you're heading for Ko Chang, there is a specifically designated stop for it between Chanthaburi and Trat. You can also get a bus to the Cambodian border crossing at Poipet, look for the bus to Aranyaprathet and tell them you are going to Poipet when you buy the ticket.

Look at the map in the next few pages

Getting In

By bus

• Northern and Northeastern Bus Terminal (Mo Chit 2 (หมอชิต 2), ☎ +66 2 9362841 (-3). The largest, busiest, and most modern terminal, replacing the old Mo Chit terminal. The upper floor serves the Isaan region in the northeast of Thailand. The ground floor serves Northern Thailand, and shares some destinations with Ekkamai (including Pattaya, Rayong, Chanthaburi and Trat). The bus terminal is a fair hike from BTS station Mo Chit or MRT station Chatuchak Park. Motorbike taxis do the trip for a fixed fare (bargaining is pointless), while tuk-tuks charge whatever they feel like — when bargaining, remember that a real taxi with air conditioning will cost you about the same as a motortaxi (assuming little traffic). You can also take Bus 77 and pay the flat fare on board (this bus also goes from the terminal via Victory Monument, Pratunam, and Silom Rd). If you have a considerable amount of luggage, the easiest, if not necessarily fastest, option is to take a taxi directly to or from the bus terminal.

Buying tickets at the terminal is reasonably easy: find a window with your destination written on it (in friendly Roman letters), pay the fare in big numbers on the same window, and you'll get a ticket on the next available departure

Getting In

By bus

Blue writing means 1st class, red means 2nd class (avoid on longer trips), and tickets for destinations in Isaan are sold from the third floor. Ask the information desk on the first floor if you need help, or any of the Transport Co. staff, easily identifiable thanks to their natty white shirts with gold buttons. Next just find the departure stall and you're on your way. If you have time to kill, there are two fairly decent air-conditioned food courts at both ends of the main terminal building, plus KFC, Dunkin' Donuts, and lots of 7-Eleven outlets. Air-conditioned buses are available directly from Bangkok Mo Chit to Siem Reap, Cambodia. Transport Co., the state-owned company running the buses, offers daily services to Siem Reap. Departures every day at 08:00 and 09:00 in both directions.

• Southern Bus Terminal (Sai Tai Mai (สายใต้ใหม่)), Phutthamonthon Sai 1 Rd, Thonburi, ☎ +66 2 894-6122. Serves all destinations west and south of Bangkok from its somewhat inconvenient location on the Thonburi side of the river.

#Rule : If you want to move in a country we recommend that you do not take buses, taxi, or trains

Getting In

By train

Railways converge on Bangkok from all parts of Thailand: from Chiang Mai in the north, Nong Khai on the Laos border, Ubon Ratchathani to the east, Aranyaprathet on the Cambodia border, Sattahip on the coast to the south, Nam Tok to the west, and Padang Besar on the Malaysia border down the peninsula to the south. Trains are run by State Railway of Thailand.

The luxurious Belmond Eastern & Oriental Express also occasionally runs between Bangkok, Kuala Lumpur and Singapore, with prices starting at US$7,500. Two runs are scheduled for late 2021.

Three high speed standard-gauge railways to Bangkok are being proposed from Kunming in China: an eastern line via Vietnam and Cambodia, a central line via Laos, and a western line via Myanmar, with further plans for the lines to continue southward into Malaysia and Singapore. As of 2021, the central line has reached Vientiane the capital of Laos, but because of COVID no trains are crossing the Chinese border. The extension of the central line to Bangkok is under construction, but completion is still years away. Work on the eastern and western routes has long stalled and completion is not remotely in sight.

Getting In

By train

• Bang Sue Station will become the terminus for all inter-city trains from Jan 2022; it's not yet known which local and regional services will also switch. You might change here for the Metro, but the place remains a work in progress. It's also connected by Bus 52 to Mo Chit, for the long distance bus terminal.

• Thonburi Train Station (ธนบุรี formerly Bangkok Noi Station) (west of the river in Thonburi). The terminus for twice-daily trains to Kanchanaburi (via Nakhon Pathom). Just to keep things confusing, the previous Thonburi Train Station right next to the river (accessible by the Chao Phraya Express Boat pier Railway Station) is now mothballed and turned into a museum, but it's only 800 m away from the new station. The weekend-only second class air conditioned tourist trains to Kanchanaburi and Nam Tok depart from Hualamphong Train Station.

• Wongwian Yai Train Station (วงเวียนใหญ่) (About 800 m from the Skytrain station of the same name. To get there, take a metered taxi or walk (using a map)). Serves the rustic Mae Klong commuter line to the fishing village of Maha Chai. Trains run roughly hourly and the trip takes about one hour.

Getting In

By train

The ride is of little interest if you want to get there fast, but is an experience for rail fans and an attraction in itself, with a nice view on the countryside's orchards, vegetable plantations and coconut groves. Maha Chai is a nice seafood destination, and if you feel like it, you can cross the Tha Chin river by ferry and continue by rail to Samut Songkhram.

By car

Getting into Bangkok by car is not a good idea, as you can easily waste half a day waiting in traffic just to get to the other side of the city. Three major highways lead to Bangkok from every direction in Thailand. The best way to get to Bangkok from Northern Thailand is via Phahonyothin Road (Rte 1), which comes from Mae Sai near the Myanmar border. Sukhumvit Road (Rte 3) comes from cities in Eastern Thailand, such as Trat, Pattaya, and Chonburi. Phetkasem Road (Rte 4), one of the longest roads in the world, extends all the way to the Malaysian border, serving Southern Thailand. To ease congestion on these highways, a new system of motorways has emerged which will be extended in the future. The New Bangkok-Chonburi Motorway (Motorway 7) connects Chonburi and Pattaya.

Getting Around

Bangkok is infamous for its congestion, but these days there are ways around it: hop on the Skytrain (BTS) and Metro (MRT) in the city centre, or use boats to navigate the city's rivers and canals. Although too expensive for the average working class Thai, the Skytrain and MRT are reasonably priced by Western standards.

Transit Bangkok will make using public transport easier by choosing the best combination of buses, MRT, BTS to get to your destination.

Skytrain

The 13 Bangkok Skytrain (BTS) (รถไฟฟ้าบีทีเอส) deserves a visit simply for the Disneyland space-ageness of it. Built in a desperate effort to ease Bangkok's insane traffic and pollution, the Skytrain covers most of the main areas of the city and is especially convenient for visiting Siam Square. There are two lines: the light green Sukhumvit Line travels along Sukhumvit Road, Siam Square and then follows Phahonyothin Road up north, where it passes Mo Chit (N8), near the Chatuchak Weekend Market, before terminating at Wat Phra Sri Mahathat (N17). In April 2017 the eastbound section crossed the border to Samut Prakan when Samrong (E15) station opened.

Getting Around

Skytrain

The dark green Silom Line starts in Petchkasem Road (Bang Wa station, S12), passes the Express Boat pier at Saphan Taksin (S6), goes through the Silom area and ends at National Stadium (W1), right next to MBK Center. Both lines come together at Siam (CEN), where you can interchange between them. Unfortunately, there is no station near Khao San Road, but you can take the Express Boat from Phra Arthit Pier to Sathorn Pier, where you can switch onto the Skytrain.

You must have 5 or 10 baht coins to purchase Skytrain tickets from vending machines, so hold on to them. At some stations there are touchscreen machines that accept 20, 50 and 100 baht notes, but there is often a queue to use them. Fares depend upon how many zones you are travelling. Consult the map (in English) near each ticket machine. If you do not have coins, queue for change from the staff at the booth. If you are in town for several days (or will make several visits during the next 30 days), weigh your options and consider:

- Rabbit card : a rechargeable stored-value card. Bring your passport when purchasing. The Rabbit card can also be used to make payments in some supermarkets
- A "ride all you like" tourist pass (140 baht/day)

Getting Around

Metro

The Metropolitan Rapid Transit (MRT) (รถไฟฟ้ามหานคร). has two lines but is being extended with construction messing up traffic in some areas. The service started as a metro (subway) train but parts of the network run now on elevated track so the label Skytrain for the BTS is becoming confusing when the Airport Rail Link also uses similar construction.

- The Blue line runs in a circle from Lak Song to Tha Phra through Thonburi, Yaowarat, Silom, Sukhumvit, Ratchadaphisek and areas around Chatuchak Weekend Market in Phahonyothin. There are interchanges to the Skytrain at Bang Wa, Si Lom, Sukhumvit and Chatuchak Park stations. The Purple Line connects Tao Poon market west of Bang Sue Train Station to points west in Nonthaburi way across Chao Phraya River.

Metro tickets are not interchangeable with BTS tickets. Fares are based on number of stations. The ticket vending machines accept coins and banknotes. Pre-paid cards of up to 1,000 baht are also available. For single ride fares, a round plastic token is used. It is electronic: simply wave it by the scanner to enter; deposit it in a slot by the exit gate leave. Children and elderly are issued tickets at half price.

Getting Around

Metro

- The Purple line is opening new areas for tourists. For example, the off-beat Siam Gypsy Junction near Tao Poon station is now much easier to access as a place where you can drink until sunrise.

Thailand's main railway connecting Bangkok to the north and northeast provinces intersects the MRT at two points: Bang Sue and Hualamphong. Those staying at Khao San Road or in the Silom or Yaowarat areas can disembark at Hualamphong for easy access to these places. However, due to the many level crossings disembarking at Bang Sue and catching the metro will take you faster even to Hualamphong although it will cost a bit more. If you are heading from the train to Suvarnabhumi airport, disembark at Bang Sue, ride the metro to Phetchaburi and switch to Airport Rail Link at Makkasan.
Metro trains run 06:00-24:00.

Getting Around

By boat

A ride on the Chao Phraya River should be high on any tourist's agenda. The cheapest and most popular option is the Chao Phraya Express Boat. , basically an aquatic bus cruising up and down the river.

The basic service goes from Wat Rajsingkorn (S4) all the way north to Nonthaburi (N30), with stops at most of Rattanakosin's major attractions including the Grand Palace (at Tha Chang) and Wat Pho (at Tha Tien). The closest pier to Khao San Road is Phra Arthit. Enter the express boat at the numerous piers and pay the conductor for the trip.

The different boat lines are indicated by the colour of the triangular pennant at the end of the boat. These flags can be confusing; don't think the yellow king's flag corresponds to the yellow line flag!

• The orange flag line (14 baht, every day 06:00-19:00) is your best bet, as it covers the major tourist areas and is fairly quick. However, it does not stop at every pier unlike the:

• Basic "no flag" line (8, 10 or 12 baht) which is fairly slow and runs only during rush hours (M-F 06:45-07:30 and M-F 16:00-16:30).

• It is better to avoid the faster yellow flag line (M-F 06:15-08:10 and M-F 15:30-18:05) since it skips many popular attractions including Khao San Road, the Grand Palace and Wat Pho.

Getting Around

By boat

• The green flag line (10, 12, 19 or 31 baht, M-F 06:10-08:10 and M-F 16:05-18:05) skips many piers but its Pakkred terminus is the closest pier to Ko Kret if you want to spend a weekday there.

By Tuk-tuk

What would Bangkok be without the much-loathed, much-loved tuk-tuks? You'll know them when you hear them, and you'll hate them when you smell them — these three-wheeled contraptions blaze around Bangkok leaving a black cloud of smog in their wake. For anything more than a 5-10 min jaunt or just the experience, they really are not worth the price — and, if you let them get away with it, the price will usually be 4 or 5 times what it should be anyway (which, for Thais, is around 30% less than the equivalent metered taxi fare).

Getting Around

By Tuk-tuk

If you still want to try the tuk-tuk, always hail a moving tuk-tuk from the main road. At tourist spots, these tuk-tuk drivers lie in waiting to disrupt your travels plans. Always agree on a price before entering the tuk-tuk. Also be crystal clear about your intended destination. If they claim that your intended destination is closed for the day, and offer to take you to other nearby tourist spots, insist on your destination or get out. If you're an all-male party, tuk-tuk drivers sometimes will just ignore your destination completely and start driving you to some brothel ("beautiful girls"). Insist continually and forcefully on going only to your destination; or take a metered taxi instead.

Getting Around

By ride share
Best choice

The main ride sharing company operating in Bangkok is Malaysian company Grab (www.grab.com/th/en/). Unlike Uber, Grab also allows you to book taxis, and gives you the option of paying your driver in cash.

By car

Bangkok is notorious for its massive traffic jams, and rightly so. In addition, traffic is chaotic and motorcyclists seemingly suicidal. Therefore, most tourists consider driving in Bangkok a nightmare, and it is recommended that you stick to public transport. However, the proliferation of massive shopping malls means that there are now places to park if you must drive into town, albeit at a high cost. Smartphones with GPS and navigation apps with voice directions make it easier to find your way.

On foot

Many of Bangkok's main attractions are within 5 km (3.1 mi) from Siam Square. Walking long distances in hot weather along busy streets can be exhausting, but is a good way to get to see the city up close. Just drink plenty of water and watch out for uneven surfaces and motorcyclists. Food leftovers and the occasional surprises left by stray animals are other reasons to look where you're going.

Attractions

Don't throw away the entry ticket of the Grand Palace, as it gives free entry to the Bang Pa-In Palace in Bang Pa-In (and not anymore to the Dusit Palace which is close to public since 2017). It is situated in a leafy, European-style area built by King Rama V to escape the heat of the Grand Palace. Its main structure is the Vimanmek Mansion, touted as the largest golden teakwood house in the world, but you could spend your whole day in the museums if you wish. There are many museums in Bangkok showing traditional Thai-style residences. Many visitors take a tour through Jim Thompson's House, the CIA-operative's mansion assembled by combining six traditional Thai-style houses near Siam Square. Ban Kamthieng in Sukhumvit, M.R. Kukrit's Heritage Home in Silom and the Suan Pakkad Palace in Phahonyothin are not quite as impressive, but still make for a nice experience. Rattanakosin's museums are mostly dedicated to history and culture, including the National Museum (about Thai history and archaeological remains), the Museum of Siam, Rattanakosin Museum (which offers two guided tours with interactive displays regarding the history of old and modern Thai life), and the King Prajadhipok Museum.

According to the divine religions, it is not permissible to visit non-heavenly temples, whatever, there are many place are more enjoyably in Bangkok and Thailand!

Attractions

Lumphini Park in Silom is the largest park in central Bangkok, and a good way to escape the fumes. Backpackers around Khao San Road can head for Santichaiprakarn Park, a small but fun park along the Chao Phraya River with a breezy atmosphere, usually with locals juggling or practicing tricks. It is built around the 18th-century Phra Sumen Fort with a nice view on the modern Rama VIII cable-stayed bridge. Zoos and animal farms are some of the more popular tourist attractions in Bangkok, but before visiting, please be aware that animal welfare in Thailand is not strictly regulated. Poor living conditions of the animals and inadequate veterinary care are examples of the sad mistreatment of the animal population. You can't go wrong at the Queen Saovabha Institute Snake Farm in Silom, as the staff takes good care of their snakes and they have a job of informing the public about the risks associated with them. Another nice family attraction is Siam Ocean World in Siam Square. It has a steep price tag, but at least you get to see the largest aquarium in Southeast Asia.

Activities

Canals trip

You can see the Chao Phraya River and the backwaters of the city by canal tour. Most of these boat trips start at the eastern bank of the Chao Phraya and then ply through the backwaters of Thonburi taking in Wat Arun, the Royal Barges National Museum, a floating market and some other minor attractions. More information about these canal tours can be found in the Thonburi article. At 1,000 baht or more, they are quite expensive. You can also negotiate a price with individual boat drivers. Damnoen Saduak is a floating market that often appears in tourist brochures of Bangkok, but in practice it is 109 km (68 mi) west of Bangkok and has to be visited by bus from the Southern Bus Terminal.

Muay Thai

Muay Thai is both a combat sport and a means of self-defence. Contestants are allowed to use almost any part of the body for fighting: feet, elbows, legs, knees and shoulders. There are two venues in Bangkok to see this sport in action: Lumpinee Boxing Stadium in Silom and Ratchadamnoen Stadium in Rattanakosin. Sessions can take the whole evening and it's not that bad if you come in slightly late as the more interesting fights tend to happen at the end.

Activities

Muay Thai

The playing of traditional style during the bouts is enjoyable as well. A downer is the steep 1,000-2,000 baht entry fee for foreigners. Thais chip in for 100 baht or less.

If you want to see Muay Thai for free, go to the MBK Fight Night outside MBK Center near Siam Square. Fights take place the last Wednesday evening of each month (starts at 18:00, lasts until around 21:00). Another option is to walk to the end of Soi Rambuttri into an alley known as Trok Kasap (near Khao San Road). Foreigners are getting classes in Muay Thai out in the open there, and many tourists generally sit on a bench in front of it to look at the action. Besides looking, this is an excellent place to do some Muay Thai yourself

Activities

Cycling

Bicycles can be rented for free in Rattanakosin, but cyclists are officially not allowed to leave the set route along the island. Even when following the route, it's still not for the faint of heart.

If renting your own bicycle, avoid the main roads and cycle through the vast system of small streets and alleys. You can cycle through the backstreets of Yaowarat, but you might want to think twice before making a turn. You can also experience life in Bangkok's countryside by cycling through green paddy fields, orchid farms and lotus fields. Bang Kachao, in brochures often referred to as the "Bangkok Jungle", is Bangkok's last green frontier. It's a semi-island across the river from Bangkok with few cars and buildings, and a great destination for cycling.

• Bangkok Biking, Baan Sri Kung 350/123, Soi 71, Rama III Rd, ☎ +66 2-285 3955. Bicycle tours in small groups to and through unseen parts of Bangkok. Mostly free of traffic. A fun excursion for the whole family. 950-2,400 baht.

• Co van Kessel, ☎ +66 2 639-7351. Many cycling tours through Bangkok, taking in Chinatown, the canals of Thonburi, the "Bangkok Jungle" and many other places in between. 950-1,950 baht.

Activities

Cycling

• Follow Me Bicycle Tours, 126 Sathorn Tai Rd, ☎ +66 2 286-5891. Half-day bicycle tours through Bangkok's residential streets. Included in the price is a fish spa and a barbecue meal after the tour. 1,000 baht.

• Grasshopper Adventures, 57 Ratchadamnoen Klang Rd (near the Democracy Monument, right around the corner from Khao San Rd), ☎ +66 2 280-0832, journeys@grasshopperadventures.com. Tours through the historic Rattanakosin district of Bangkok, to the outskirts of Bangkok and one that takes place at night. 1,000-1,600 baht.

• SpiceRoads, 45 Soi Pannee, Pridi Banomyong Soi 26, Sukhumvit Soi 71, ☎ +66 2 381-7490. Many one and multi-day cycling trips in and around Bangkok. There are trips to the Bangkok Jungle, Ko Kret, Yaowarat, and Thonburi. 2,950 baht.

Food

Bangkok boasts a stunning 50,000 places to eat; not only thousands of Thai restaurants, but a wide selection of world-class international cuisine too. With the rise of the expat community and high expenditure for local Thais, Bangkok has fast become a gastronomical paradise. Prices are generally high by Thai standards, but cheap by international standards. A good meal is unlikely to cost more than 300 baht, although there are a few restaurants (primarily in hotels) where you can easily spend 10 times this. Sukhumvit is known for many of popular restaurants but the business district of Silom is now littered with many of Bangkok's top dining destinations. Practically every cuisine in the world is represented here, be it French, Lebanese, Mexican, Vietnamese, or fusion combining many of these together in a quirky, but delicious mix. Bangkok's Italian town is Soi Ton Son near Siam Square. Of course, for those on a budget, street stalls abound with simple Thai dishes at around 30 baht. There are especially plenty of budget restaurants in Khao San Road.

Food

There are plenty of vegetarian restaurants in the more tourist-friendly parts of town (especially in hippie district Khao San Road). Vegetarian dishes are also readily available on the menus of regular restaurants. On request, even typical street restaurants will easily cook a vegetarian equivalent of a popular Thai dish for you. Ask for "jay" food to leave the meat out of the dish. For example, "khao pad" is fried rice and "khao pad jay" is vegetarian fried rice. For vegans, the most common animal product used would be oyster sauce. To avoid it, say "mai ao naam man hoi". Be aware that all street noodle vendors use meat broth for noodle soup.

Food

Street food

While generally not particularly high class, street food is among the most delicious food and there even is a venue that earned a Michelin star in their 2018 guide. The venues can be found all over Bangkok—wherever you're staying, you rarely have to walk more than 100 m for a cart or street restaurant. Many street vendors sell satay (สะเต๊ะ) with hot sauce for 5-10 baht a piece. Khao San Road is known for its carts selling bugs—yes, insects. They are deep fried, nutritious and quite tasty with the soy sauce that is sprayed on them. Types available: scorpions, water beetles, grasshoppers, crickets, bamboo larvae, mealworms and some seasonal specialties. Break off the legs from grasshoppers and crickets or they will get stuck in your throat.

Around the corner from Khao San Road in front of the department store and supermarkets the street is lined with a myriad stalls selling all manner of tempting delicacies: sweets and crackers, coconut jellies, candied fruits, fish balls on skewers, tamarind sweets dipped in chili and sugar and a host of other delights.

Sleep

Bangkok has a vast range of accommodation, including some of the best hotels in the world — but also some of the worst dives. Broadly speaking, Khao San Road is backpacker city; the riverside of Silom and Thonburi is home to The Oriental and The Peninsula respectively, often ranked among the best in the world, and priced to match. Most of the city's moderate and expensive hotels can be found in Siam Square, Sukhumvit and Silom, though they also have their share of budget options.

When choosing your digs, think of the amount of luxury you want to pay for — air-conditioning can be advised, as temperatures don't drop below 20 °C (68 °F) at night. Also pay careful attention to Skytrain, metro and express boat access, as a well-placed station or pier could make your stay in Bangkok much more comfortable. In general, accommodation in Bangkok is cheap. It's possible to have a decent double room with hot shower and air-conditioning for about 500 baht/night. If you want more luxury, expect to pay around 1,500 baht for a double room in the main tourist areas. Even staying at one of Bangkok's top hotels only costs around 5,000 baht — the price of a standard double room in much of Europe.

Bangkok, Thailand

Safety

Please read this section with carefully!

Given its size, Bangkok is surprisingly safe, with violent crimes like mugging and robbery unusual. One of the biggest dangers are motorbikes who ride on pavements at speed, go through red lights, undertake buses as they stop to let passengers off and generally drive far too fast especially through stationary traffic. If you are going to hire a bike, make sure you have insurance in case you are injured. You may be the world's best driver but you'll meet many of the world's worst drivers in Thailand.

Bangkok does have more than its fair share of scams, and many individuals in the tourist business do not hesitate to overcharge unwary visitors. As a rule of thumb, it is wise to decline all offers made by someone who appears to be a friendly local giving a hapless tourist some local advice. Short-changing tourists is reasonably common as well, don't hesitate to complain if you are not given the correct change.

Never get in a tuk-tuk if someone else is trying to get you into one. Most Bangkok locals do not approach foreigners without an ulterior motive

Safety

Scam

You should always be on the look-out for scammers, especially in major tourist areas. There are dozens of scams in Bangkok, but by far the most widely practiced is the gem scam. Always beware of tuk-tuk drivers offering all-day tours for prices as low as 10 baht. You may indeed be taken on a full-day tour, but you will end up only visiting one gem and souvenir shop after another. Don't buy any products offered by pushy salespeople — the "gems" are pretty much always worthless pieces of cut glass and the suits are of deplorable quality. The tuk-tuk driver gets a commission if you buy something — and fuel coupons even if you don't. Unless the idea of travelling by tuk-tuk appeals to you, it's almost always cheaper, more comfortable and less hassle to take a metered taxi.

Be highly skeptical when an English-speaking Thai at a popular tourist attraction approaches you out of the blue, telling that your intended destination is closed or offering discount admissions. Temples are almost always free (the main exceptions are Wat Phra Kaeo and Wat Pho) and open just about every day of the year.

Safety

Scam

Be highly skeptical when an English-speaking Thai at a popular tourist attraction approaches you out of the blue, telling that your intended destination is closed or offering discount admissions. Temples are almost always free (the main exceptions are Wat Phra Kaeo and Wat Pho) and open just about every day of the year. Anyone telling you otherwise, even if they have an official-looking identification card, is most likely out to scam you, especially if they suggest a tuk-tuk ride to some alternate sights to see until the sight re-opens. At paid admission sites, verify the operating hours at the ticket window.

> What to do if you fall for the gem scam?
> As long as you're still in Thailand, it's not too late. Contact the Tourist Authority of Thailand, ☎ +66 2 694-1222 or the Tourist Police, ☎ 1155 immediately, file a police report, and return to the store to claim a refund — they must, by law, return 80%. If your gems have been mailed, contact the Bangkok Mail Centre, ☎ +66 2 215-0966 (-195) immediately and ask them to track your package; they'll find it if you act fast, and know the name, address and date it was mailed.

Safety

In general, never ask a taxi driver for a recommendation for something. They will likely take you to a dubious place where they get a commission. In particular, do not ask a taxi driver for a restaurant recommendation. An infamous place taxi drivers take unsuspecting tourists is Somboon D, which is a terrible seafood restaurant in a seedy area under the train tracks on Makkasan Road (☎ +66 2 6527-7667). A typical meal there costs 800 baht per person and it comes with little seafood, no service and complaints are not taken by the management. Also beware of private bus companies offering direct trips from Bangkok to other cities with "VIP" buses. There are a lot of scams performed by these private bus companies. The so-called direct VIP trips may end up changing three or four uncomfortable minibuses to the destination, and the 10-11-hour trip may well turn into 17–18 hr. Instead, try to book public Transport Co. buses from the main bus terminals. It's worth the extra shoe-leather, as there have been reports of robberies on private buses as well.

Please for more information, try to contact us via e-mail!

Bangkok, Thailand

Safety

As elsewhere in Thailand, be careful with what you eat. Outside of major tourist hotels and resorts, stay away from raw leafy vegetables, egg-based dressings like mayonnaise, unpackaged ice cream and minced meat as hot weather tends to make food go bad faster. In short, stick to boiled, baked, fried or peeled goods.

Tap water in Bangkok is said to be safe when it comes out the plant, but unfortunately the plumbing along the way often is not, so it's wise to avoid drinking the stuff, even in hotels. Any water served to you in good restaurants will at least be boiled, but it's better to order sealed bottles instead, which are available everywhere at low prices.

Take care with ice, which may be made with tap water of questionable potability as above. Some residents claim that ice with round holes is made by commercial ice makers who purify their water; others state that it is wise not to rely on that claim.

"It is very important to travel with other people in Thailand, because it is difficult to move around on your own"

Internet

Due to the surge of mobile connectivity, Internet cafés are not common as they used to be. If you look carefully, you may find them in tourist districts such as Khao San Road for around 30-60 baht per hour.

Many cafés and pubs do offer free Wi-Fi to their customers, including the ubiquitous Coffee World chain in all of its branches; ask staff for the password. TrueMove offers both free and paid Wi-Fi access. If you want to get online for free, you must register first, and both session and time is limited. Their network is accessible in many malls, including Siam Square, and sometimes can be available from your room if you stay in a nearby hot-spot — just look for the 'truewifi' network, you can register. Most hotels and guest houses provide free Wi-Fi.

There is not a lot of free Wi-Fi available in old districts like Rattanakosin or Yaowarat. Even at McDonald's and Starbucks, Wi-Fi is not free or not available at all.

If you are staying for more than a couple of days and prefer to stay connected without being limited to hotspots, a prepaid SIM card with mobile data is a good option. Being able to use a smartphone for navigation and reviews is very useful in a city where recommendations and directions offered by locals are not always reliable. See the Telephone section for details.

Telephone

The area code for Bangkok is 02. You only need to dial the 0 if you're calling from within Thailand. Pay phones are not commonplace, as most Thais have a mobile phone. If you want to avoid high roaming costs, you can buy a local SIM card for 100 baht at Suvarnabhumi Airport or mobile phone shops throughout the city. The 100 baht is not just for the SIM card, but is immediately your first pre-paid amount. Topping it up is easy, such as at 7-Eleven convenience stores. Making international calls is also cheaper this way.
As of July 2014, the True booth at Suvarnabhumi Airport is offering free tourist Sim cards preloaded with 10 baht calling credit as well as 20 MB of 3G access.

Medical care

Many people go to Bangkok to undergo medical treatments that are a fraction of the cost charged in their home countries. While public hospitals can be understaffed and overcrowded with long wait times, private hospitals are among the best in the world. The best-regarded, and most expensive (though still affordable by Western standards), is Bumrungrad International Hospital, which attracts about 400,000 foreign patients per year or an average of 1,000+ a day. There are also other hospitals, such as Samitivej, Bangkok Hospital and BNH Hospital, that specialize in serving foreigners.

Photo Gallery

Photo Gallery

Bangkok, Thailand

Photo Gallery

Bangkok, Thailand

Photo Gallery

Khao Sok National Park

One of the most beautiful wildlife reserves in Thailand

Khao Sok National Park, Thailand

Overview

Many people go to Bangkok to undergo medical treatments that are a fraction of the cost charged in their home countries. While public hospitals can be understaffed and overcrowded with long wait times, private hospitals are among the best in the world. The best-regarded, and most expensive (though still affordable by Western standards), is Bumrungrad International Hospital, which attracts about 400,000 foreign patients per year or an average of 1,000+ a day. There are also other hospitals, such as Samitivej, Bangkok Hospital and BNH Hospital, that specialize in serving foreigners.

Khao Sok National Park, Thailand

Learn more

There are 2 main sections of Khao Sok National Park. The west entrance is where Park HQ is located along with the main hiking trails. The east entrance is where Ratchaprapha Pier is located where you go to get to the floating rafthouses. The 2 entrances are 65 km apart and over 1 hour of driving, so please take that into consideration when planning your trip.

"Khao Sok" is used as a catch-all term to describe the general area where the park is located. This usually includes the area from Ratchaprapha Pier west to the Surat Thani -Phangnga border, along Highway 401. "Khao Sok Village" is the 2km stretch of road from Highway 401 to Park HQ. "Khlong Sok" is both the name of the river in the area as well at the administrative subdistrict (ตำบล คลองศก).

• Khao Sok National Park HQ. Khao Sok National Park entrance. Hiking trails, camping, and visitor center.

• Rajjaprabha Dam Pier (Cheow Lan Lake Pier). This is the boat pier to the floating rafthouses.

Khao Sok National Park, Thailand

Geography

Beautiful sandstone and mudstone rocks rise about 300–600 m (984–1,969 ft) above sea level. The park is traversed by a limestone mountain range from north to south with a high point of 950 m (3,117 ft). This mountain range is hit by monsoon rain coming from both the Gulf of Thailand and the Andaman Sea, which makes it among Thailand's wettest regions with an annual rain fall of 3,500 mm (137.8 in). Heavy rainfall and falling leaves led to the erosion of the limestone rocks and created the significant karst formations seen today.

Khao Sok National Park, Thailand

Geography

Bamboo holds topsoil very tenaciously, preventing soil erosion on hillsides and riverbanks. With more than 1,500 species, bamboo is the oldest grass in the world, dating back nearly 60 million years. Liana trees grow rapidly wrapping around any vertical or horizontal support base such as takian or "rain trees". Thus, it's dangerous to simply cut a tree in the jungle because it can pull connected liana vines with it creating a cascade of damage. Buttress roots are enlarged root bases mostly of trees that grow above the upper canopy. The theory about these roots is that they either developed in order to be more grounded in storms and rain or that they spread out on the ground in order to get more nutrients.

Many kinds of wild fruit can be found around the national park and serve as sustenance for animals. Among those fruits are wild jackfruit, mangosteen, durian, rambutan, jujube, pomelo, and wild bananas. Wild pepper and ginger are not uncommon. Khao Sok National Park is perhaps most famous for the bua phut (Rafflesia kerrii) flower.

Khao Sok National Park, Thailand

Wildlife

The park is estimated to contain over five percent of the world's species. Wild mammals include Malayan tapir, Asian elephant, tiger, sambar deer, bear, gaur, banteng, serow, wild boar, pig-tailed macaque, langur, white handed gibbons, squirrel, muntjak, mouse deer, and barking deer.

The world's only known amphibious centipede, Scolopendra cataracta, was discovered on a stream bank near the national park in 2001.

Climate

The so-called wet season is between late April–December. The temperature ranges from 22–36 °C (72–97 °F) all year around. Humidity and warm temperature provide the optimal environment for a rich eco-system in this tropical rain forest.

Khao Sok National Park, Thailand

Map

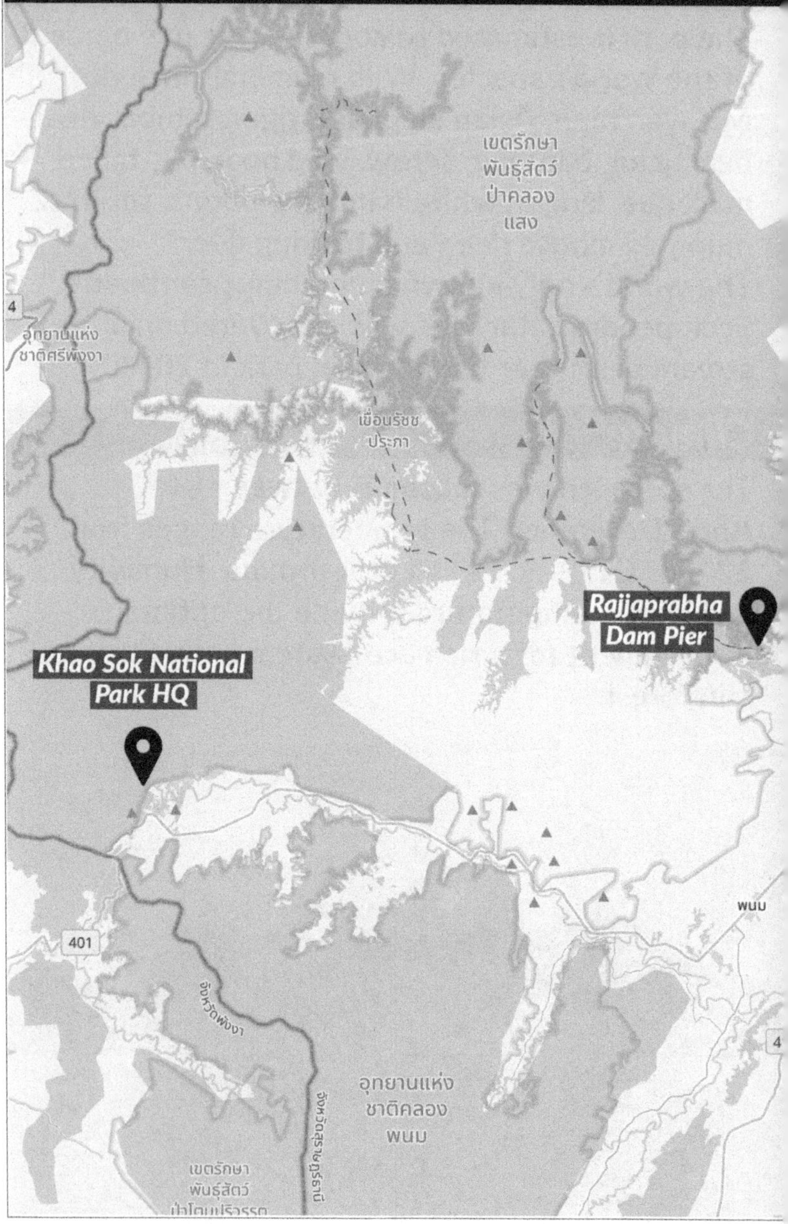

เขตรักษา
พันธุ์สัตว์
ป่าคลอง
แสง

4

อุทยานแห่ง
ชาติศรีพังงา

เขื่อนรัชช
ประภา

Rajjaprabha Dam Pier

Khao Sok National Park HQ

401

พนม

4

อุทยานแห่ง
ชาติคลอง
พนม

เขตรักษา
พันธุ์สัตว์
ป่าโตนเจริญ

Khao Sok National Park, Thailand

Getting In

● *By plane*

The closest airport is Surat Thani International Airport (URT). There are multiple flights daily from Bangkok (DMK IATA and BKK IATA) and Chiang Mai (CNX IATA).

● Surat Thani International Airport (URT IATA), 73 Moo 3, Hua Toei, Phunphin district (64km east of Ratchaprapha Pier; 105km east of Khao Sok National Park HQ).

- Domestic

● Air Asia, ☎ 2-515-9999 (domestic). Flights from Bangkok (Don Mueang Airport), and Chiang Mai.

● Nok Air, ☎ 1318. Flights from Bangkok (Don Mueang Airport).

● Thai Lion Air, ☎ 2-529-9999 (domestic), info@lionairthai.com. Flights from Bangkok (Don Mueang Airport).

● Thai Smile, ☎ 02-118-8888 (domestic), customer.service@thaismileair.com. Flights from Bangkok (Suvarnabhumi Airport).

Once you arrive in Surat Thani, there are buses or minivans to Khao Sok with Phantip Travel. Only buy the tickets directly from operator you are using. There is a Tourism kiosk at the airport, but they sell bus, minivan, and ferry tickets at inflated prices.

Khao Sok National Park, Thailand

Getting In

• By plane

Phantip Office - Surat Thani Airport Branch, Sura
Thani International Airport (Ground Floor, beside
exit), ☎ +66 77-272-230, +66 77-282-331,
info@phantiptravel.com. edit
Surat Thani (Airport) – Ratchaprapha Dam (1.3
hrs, 250 baht)
Surat Thani (Airport) – Khao Sok (2 hrs, 250 baht)
Car rentals are also available at the airport.

• By Bus

- From Surat Thani:
Minibus service: departure every hour from
07:30 till 17:30 (but the last one can be
cancelled).
• Phantip Office - Suratthani Town Branch,
293/6-8 Talad Mai Road, Muang Surat Thani, ☎
+66 77-272-230, +66 77-282-331,
info@phantiptravel.com. edit
Surat Thani (Town) – Ratchaprapha Dam (2 hrs,
250 baht)
Surat Thani (Town) – Khao Sok (2.5 hrs, 250 baht)
Bus running approximately every hour. Transit
time is about 2.5 hours. Price: about 120 baht.
• Talad Kaset 2 (Downtown Transportation Hub),
Talad Mai Road, Muang Surat Thani.

Khao Sok National Park, Thailand

Getting In

The closest major train station is the Surat Thani Railway Station in Phunphin district.

● Surat Thani Railway Station (สถานีรถไฟสุราษฎร์ธานี), Phunphin District, Surat Thani.

Once you arrive in Surat Thani, there are minivans to Khao Sok with Phantip Travel.

● Phantip Office - Surat Thani Train Station Branch, ☎ +66 77-272-230, +66 77-282-331, info@phantiptravel.com.

● Surat Thani (Train Station) – Khao Sok (3 hrs, 200 baht)

● Surat Thani (Train Station) – Ratchaprapha Dam (3.3 hrs, 200 baht)

Khao Sok National Park, Thailand

Map

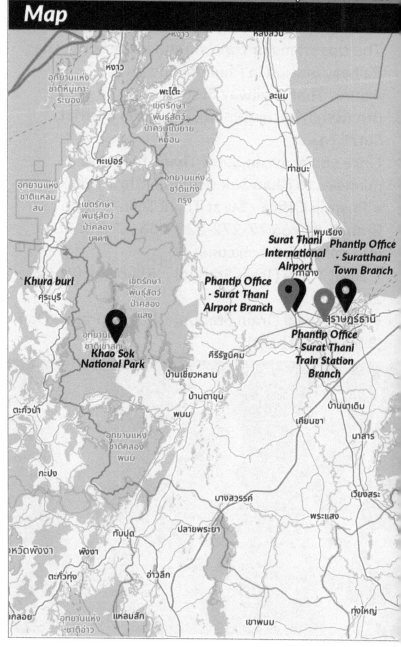

Khao Sok National Park, Thailand

Fees and permits

Foreigners: 300 baht for adults, 150 baht for children; Thais: 40 baht for adults, 20 baht for children.

Upon presentation of a Pink Thai ID Card/Yellow Tabien Baan or Thai Work Permit, the fee may be reduced to the Thai rate at the gatekeeper's discretion. A Thai Driver's Licence is no longer valid ID at national parks but you may still be able to get the Thai rate with it.

Buy your admission at the park entrance. Tickets are valid for 24 hours only. If you plan on visiting Park HQ and the lake on the same day, keep your admission ticket so you don't have to pay the entrance fee again. Some tours will include the park entrance fee in the tour package, something to take into consideration when choosing a tour.

Getting Around

Walking is the primary mode of transportation, as the road to the park is 2 km and the farthest one can walk into the park is about 20 km. There are motorbike and bicycle rentals available near Park HQ if you want to explore the surrounding area.

Khao Sok National Park, Thailand

Attractions

- Inside Park HQ
- Khao Sok National Park Visitor Center.
- Western Track

The Western Track is also known as Route 1: Bang Hua Rat Waterfall - Ton Kloi Waterfall Nature Trail or the Wide Trail. The route covers 9 km which visitors can walk on their own. The trail is usually closed past Wang Yao, yearly from 1 June - 14 December, due to the rainy season (ie. dangerous conditions). You may be able to hire a guide to go further.

- Bang Hua Rat Waterfall (น้ำตก บางหัวแรด, Bang Hua Raed Waterfall). Popular for rafting activities, this waterfall with small rapids is 3km from the visitor center.
- Bang Leiap Nam Waterfall (วังยาว). Closed yearly from 1 Jun - 14 Dec.
- Than Sawan Waterfall (น้ำตก ธารสวรรค์). Closed yearly from 1 Jun - 14 Dec. This waterfall rushes down over a sheer cliff, like a rainbow curve, into Khlong Sok. It is about 9 km from the Park's headquarters, or around 3 km from Tang Nam.
- Ton Kloi Waterfall (น้ำตก โตนกลอย). Closed yearly from 1 Jun - 14 Dec. Namtok Ton Kloi originates from Khlong Sok. It is a one-tiered waterfall with a stony ground for visitors to take a rest beside it. It is about 9 km from the Park's headquarters.

Khao Sok National Park, Thailand

Map

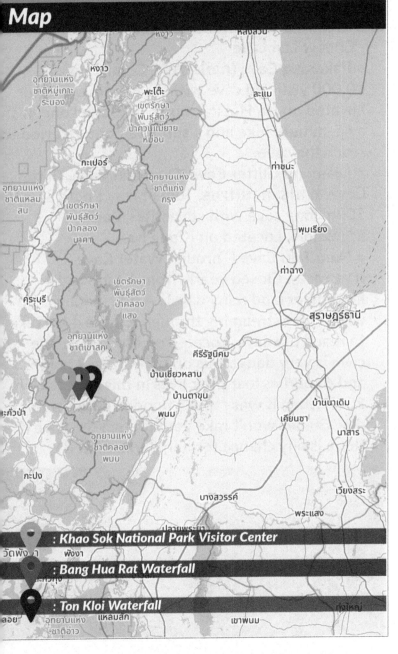

: *Khao Sok National Park Visitor Center*

: *Bang Hua Rat Waterfall*

: *Ton Kloi Waterfall*

Khao Sok National Park, Thailand

Attractions

- Cheow Lan Lake
- Pakarang Cave (ถ้ำปะการัง, Coral Cave). A 10,000 year-old cave with a cavernous interior. Located on Ha Hoi Rai, north of Klong Long. It's a 45-minute hike and a short bamboo raft ride to reach the cave.
- Diamond Glitter Cave (Diamond Cave, Glitter Cave, ถ้ำประกายเพชร, Tum Prakay Phet). Small, 100m long cave with stalactites. Easily accessible. Located on Klong Ka.
- Nam Talu Cave (Through Water Cave, ถ้ำน้ำทะลุ). Closed yearly from 1 June to 14 December (and rainy days).. A 500 m long cave with water streaming through it. It's a 4 km hike to reach the cave. Located on Klong Pey. The cave is very dangerous on rainy days. 2 guides and 6 tourists lost their lives in this cave back in 2007 when it was rapidly flooded during a rainy day. Guides won't take you through the cave if there is any chance for rain during that day.

: *Nam Talu Cave*

: *Diamond Glitter Cave*

: *Pakarang Cave*

Khao Sok National Park, Thailand

Activities

Khao Sok National Park has various activities for tourists who enjoy activities such as trekking, canoeing, bamboo rafting. A boat tour to Cheow Lan lake is also available.

• Trekking : Due to Khao Sok being a tropical rainforest, there are many wild animals such as "wild elephants, serow, tigers, Malayan sun bears and over 180 bird species to watch". Those interested in trekking can hire a local guide. Rafflesia Kerrii Meijer can be found in the area. Tourists may stay in the rainforest overnight.

• Canoeing and Bamboo rafting : Sok River is known for beautiful views along the river. There are local guides for tourists to hire for canoeing and bamboo rafting tours.

• Boat to Cheow Lan lake : Within the deep forest, there are caves to explore such as Diamond cave, Khang Cow Cave and Nam Talu cave which connect to Cheow Lan lake. Nam Talu cave is about 12 km (7.5 mi) from the headquarters of Khao Sok National Park. Tour guides are available to boat visitors from the waterfall to the lake.

Khao Sok National Park, Thailand

Food

Most guesthouses have a restaurant. Meals are usually 70-100 baht; cuisines are limited to Thai and European dishes. The standard of hygiene across all establishments is high, however if you are concerned look for places displaying the Clean Food, Good Taste sign. This appellation is bestowed by the government on restaurants that maintain a high standard of cleanliness and food preparation.

All restaurants have fresh fruit and fruit juices or shakes (fruit blended with ice). Convenience stores often sell bananas and other fresh fruit outside their establishments. Depending on the season, you will see in the trees and for sale a variety of fruit, including rambutan, longan, pomelo, mango, mangosteen, a few varieties of banana, papaya, and guava.

● The Misty Restaurant at Morning Mist Resort, 53/3 M.6 T.Klong Sok, ☎ +66 623 370607, morningmistresort@gmail.com. 07.15-21.00. Outstanding view of the mountain and the garden. (Since Oct 2019)

Khao Sok National Park, Thailand

Sleep

- Inside Park HQ :

There are several kinds of accommodations through the National Park available at Park Headquarters. You can book via the Visitor Center onsite or through the DNP website.

- Bungalow rentals: 800-1,000 baht per unit
- Tent rentals: 150 - 600 baht per tent
- Youth Hostel: 100 baht per person
- Campsite Rental: 50 baht per person (bring your own tent - 30 baht for campsite + 20 baht for overnight fee = 50฿ baht)

- Near Park HQ :

There is one main road in Khao Sok where all of the guesthouses are located. They all offer similar style accommodation (mainly bungalows). Price: 200-2,500 baht. Most have restaurants, Internet, and a travel agency. Even in peak season it shouldn't be difficult to find accommodation.

- The Cliff and River Jungle Resort, 251 หมู่ที่ 7 Khlong Sok, Phanom District, ☎ +6677913050. Check-out: 12:00. Pool. 2,000-5,500 baht. (Since Oct 2022)

- Khao Sok Nature Resort (Opposite Art's River View). Run by Mr Tee and Mrs Ae, it was the first tree house accommodation in Khao Sok. The property is huge and contains a restaurant, fruit garden, orchid garden, etc. It is framed by limestone cliffs and a river. 700-1,500 baht.

Khao Sok National Park, Thailand

Sleep

● **Khao Sok Paradise Resort**, 119 Khlong Sok, Phanom District, ☎ +66 83 3061044, Check-in: 14:00. Chill jungle resort with wifi, A/C & included breakfast. 700-3,800 baht. (Since Oct 2022)

● **Khao Sok Rainforest Resort**, 122 Moo 6 Klongsok (On the left side of Khao Sok Bridge. The distance from Rte 401 at km109 to the resort is approximately 2.5 km), ☎ +66 898 276230, Lies along two streams in which you can swim and enjoy nature. Several types of rooms: riverside bungalows, mountain side bungalows, tree houses, and family rooms. Bungalows have some great views of the jungle-covered mountains alive with colour and sounds. A certified tour operator and resort registered with the Tourism Authority of Thailand (TAT). 500-2,500 baht.

● **Khao Sok River Lodge**, 55/779-780 Villa Daowroong Village, ☎ +66 89 7252244, +66 89 7252277, info@khaosokriverlodge.com. 1,200-2,500 baht breakfast included.

Please for more suggestions contact us!

Khao Sok National Park, Thailand

Map

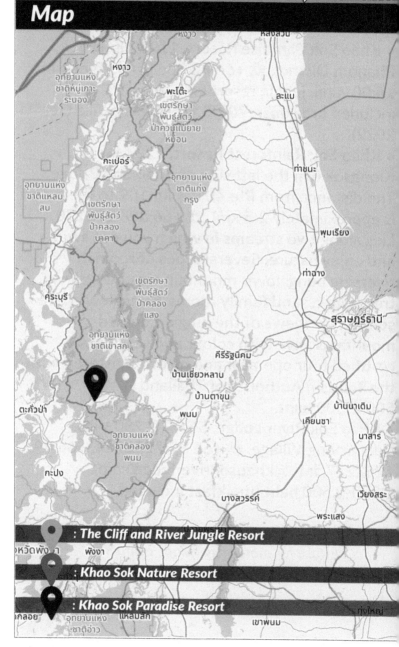

: The Cliff and River Jungle Resort

: Khao Sok Nature Resort

: Khao Sok Paradise Resort

Khao Sok National Park, Thailand

Photo Gallery

Khao Sok National Park, Thailand

Photo Gallery

Khao Sok National Park, Thailand

Photo Gallery

Khao Sok National Park, Thailand

Photo Gallery

Photo Gallery

Phuket

The original Thai paradise island,
now very developed but with
some still beautiful beaches

Phuket, Thailand

Overview

Phuket (ภูเก็ต), "puh-KET", is Thailand's largest island. It is 48 km in length, 21 km at its widest, and is in Southern Thailand, on the west-facing Andaman Sea coastline, suspended from the southern tip of Phang Nga province by a pair of short but substantial road bridges.

Overview

Cities

- Phuket Town — the administrative centre of the province with the cheapest accommodation,
- Cape Panwa — home to Phuket Aquarium
- Chalong Bay — home to Phuket's most popular yacht anchorage and the primary gateway to the islands off Phuket
- Karon — the second most-developed beach after Patong, split into Karon Yai and Karon Noi Beaches
- Laem Sing — small bay with stunning views, between Kamala and Surin Beaches
- Mai Khao — many posh resorts, Thai villages, and restaurants, very quiet and far away from it all
- Patong — the largest and most popular beach resort known for its nightlife
- Rawai — jumping off point for lots of local islands, popular with locals for eating on the beach
- Surin — an up-and-coming upmarket destination

Map

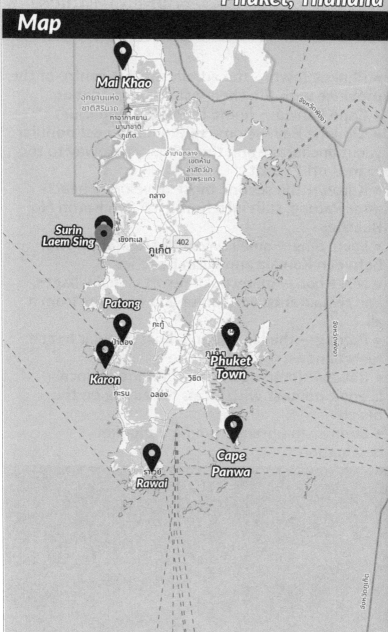

Overview

Attractions

• Ko Maphrao — fishery villages, walking along nature trails, fishing and biking

• Ko Lon — quiet, mostly Muslim island with a few bungalows

• Ko Mai Thon — gorgeous little island with only one (expensive) place to stay

• Ko Racha — two islands (Yai and Noi), popular with scuba divers and a relaxing snorkelling destination

• Ko Sire — sea Gypsy colony, connected to the mainland by a causeway

• Phra Taew National Park — Phuket's last significant virgin rain forest

Map

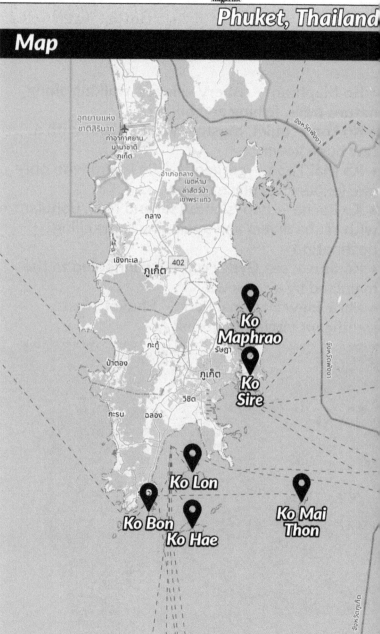

Phuket, Thailand

Overview

Beaches

- **Bang Thao** : long, very quiet beach.
- **Kamala** : a quieter beach to the north of Patong.
- **Kata** : busy, clean tourist beach with good surf, also includes Kata Noi, its quieter sister.
- **Nai Thon and Nai Yang**: two quiet beaches in Sirinat National Park
- **Nai Han** : somewhat quieter beach (probably the best) in the south, near Laem Phromthep view point.
- **Ya Nui** : good snorkelling on a shallow reef that juts out from the beach.

Phuket, Thailand

Map

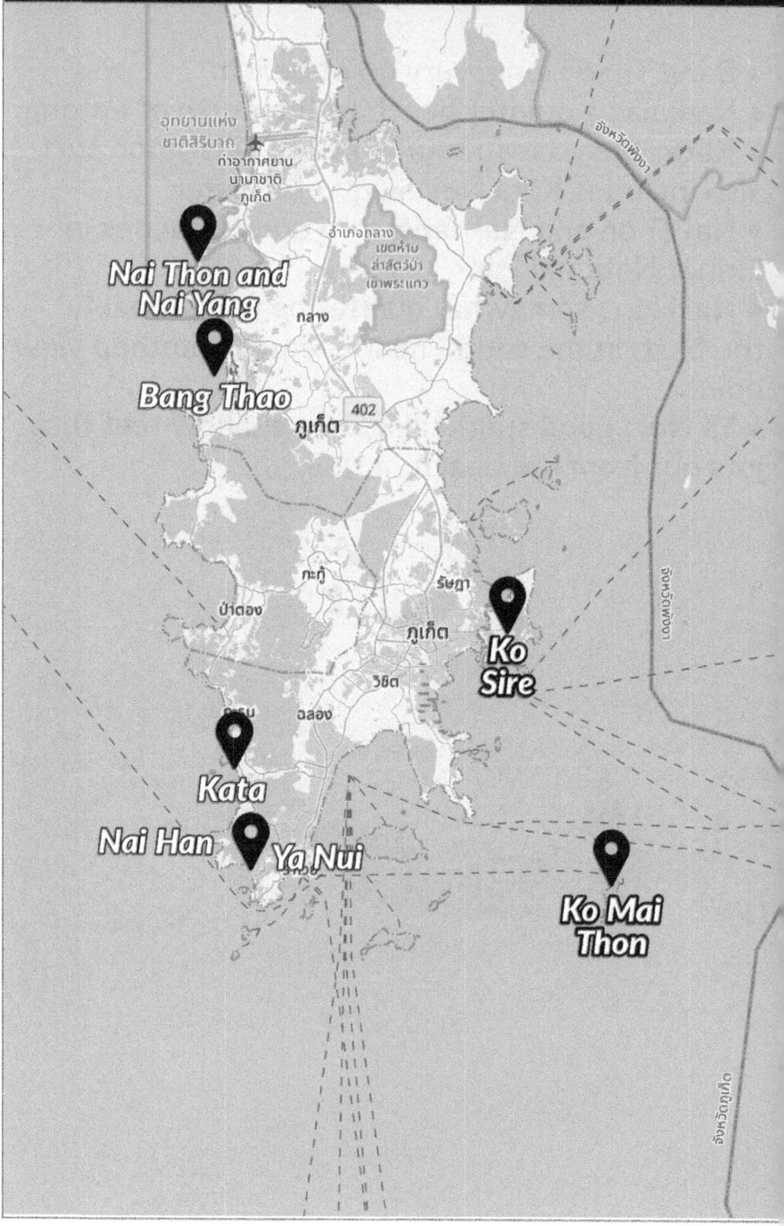

Phuket, Thailand

Learn more

Phuket floats in balmy Andaman Sea waters on Thailand's Indian Ocean coastline, 862 km south of Bangkok.

Phuket used to derive its wealth from tin and rubber, and enjoys a rich and colourful history. The island was on one of the major trading routes between India and China, and was frequently mentioned in foreign traders' ship's logs.

Phuket's top earner now is tourism, which has transformed the island into Thailand's wealthiest province. Expect prices to be a bit higher than on the mainland.

The west coast of Phuket was hit severely by the Indian Ocean tsunami of December 2004, but almost no evidence of the damage remains.

Phuket enjoys great popularity as a travel destination. Most beaches are on the west coast, with Phuket Town to the southeast and the airport in the north

Climate

Phuket is hot and humid throughout the year. The hot season is generally considered to be from Mar to early May. During the summer monsoon season from May-Oct, mornings and afternoons are sunny and clear, but it tends to rain in the evenings and water clarity goes down. Locals consider Nov-Feb the "cool" season, and the weather is quite tolerable.

Phuket, Thailand

Getting In

● by plane

Phuket International Airport (HKT IATA) (is in the northwest of the island). This compact airport is Thailand's second largest hub, second only to Bangkok.

There are very frequent flights from Bangkok and direct flights to many other airports in the region, including Kuala Lumpur, Singapore, Jakarta and direct charters to Europe and Australia in the high season. Kuala Lumpur, Singapore and also Jakarta tourists usually step directly to Phuket without step on Bangkok at all, due to distance of Bangkok to Phuket is relatively same with distance of Kuala Lumpur to Phuket. Backpackers can go to Bangkok from Phuket with 12 hours night buses, if necessary.

The airport is notionally divided into Terminals 1 and 2, with some charter and low-cost operators using the second, but these are only a short distance apart and connected by an air-conditioned walkway.

Domestic flights

Thai Airways flies from Bangkok's Suvarnabhumi Airport several times every day, and once daily from Chiang Mai (but there are no direct flights in the opposite direction). Additionally, they sell tickets from/to many domestic and international destinations with stopovers in Bangkok, which are usually cheaper (especially international) than if you book separate tickets.

Getting In

● Domestic Flights

Worth checking if you book just a few days before flight, as low-cost airlines may cost just a few less in this situation, but you get world-famous Thai Airways service.

Air Asia fly from Phuket to Chiang Mai direct, twice a day at 10:35 and 19:20, affording an opportunity to combine a beach holiday with experiencing the wildlife and exotic cultures of northern Thailand. From Chiang Mai to Phuket flights depart at 13:00 and 21:45. They fly from two cities in Isaan as well, daily from Udon Thani (handy for a trip into Laos) and four times per week from Ubon Ratchathani.

Bangkok Airways has a monopoly on direct flights between Phuket and U-Tapao (Pattaya/Sattahip) and Ko Samui. They also have 6 daily flights from Bangkok. Fares are usually the same as Thai Airways, but sometimes they have very inexpensive promotional fares.

Thai Airways International and Bangkok Airways fly to Suvarnabhumi (pronounced: soo-Var-na-phoom), whereas Nok Air and Orient Thai fly from Don Mueang Airport. This may be of importance when you have a connecting flight.

Getting In

Airport transport

To get from the airport to your destination, there are several options :

• **Private bus service**

A private bus service runs between the airport and Patong and the reverse. There is not yet an English-language website for this service. Times and fares are unclear. There are reportedly signs directing passengers to the curbside bus, but it is not easy to find (Since Oct 2013).

• **Municipal airport bus**

It's air conditioned andoperates daily 06:30-20:4 every 60-90 min. To Phuket Town bus station costs 100 baht (Since Apr 2016) and takes one hour. Local buses run from there and Ranong St Market to all the major beaches until around 18:00. After getting off a bus just cross the street and wait for the continuing bus there. It is a very convenient and comfortable spot, with no touts hustlers, plenty of shade and a minimart for drink and snacks. The bus will stop anywhere along its route upon signalling the driver ("bus hiking"). Se Airport Bus Phuket.

If you are going to take the municipal airport bus from Phuket to the airport in the afternoon (especially the 16:30 and 17:30 buses) you shoul allow yourself plenty of time. With dozens of schoolchildren getting on and off during weekday and/or congested traffic the bus is frequently delayed en route.

Getting In

• By train

There are no direct train services to Phuket. But many trains leave from Bangkok central station going south all the way to Singapore. The most comfortable are the sleeper trains. Travellers by train must get off at Phun Phin railway station in Surat Thani Province and continue for another 5 hours by regular bus to Phuket. Do not buy the bus ticket until you actually see the bus and can make sure it is not standing room only, as it picks up passengers at the popular Ko Samui ferry. If full, wait for the next one.

• By bus

Buses to mainland destinations including Bangkok, Chumphon, Hat Yai, Krabi, Phang Nga, Ranong, Satun, Sungai Kolok and Surat Thani use the BKS terminal off Phang Nga Rd in Phuket Town. The most reliable buses from Bangkok are the public BKS buses from the Southern Bus Terminal to Phuket. The journey takes 13 hours. There are also some private bus companies, Phuket Travel Tour, Phuket Central Tour, and Phuket Travel Service . Khao San Road operations have a bad reputation for theft, often turn out to include a "surprise" transfer to a minibus at Surat Thani, and are best avoided. Richly Travel Center offers a bus leaving at 19:00 from near the Hualampong Train Station inside Bangkok (without having to transfer to the Southern Bus Terminal). The TAT next door offers the same.

Getting In

• By bus

From Phuket bus terminal to your final destination, you can take a motorcycle taxi, tuk-tuk, meter-taxi, or bus.

Before exiting the Phuket bus terminal, grab a free Phuket map from the information window. While supplies may always not be on hand, the map is a great way to get your bearing before jumping-off.

"We apologize, we did not include some paragraphs, because they may confuse the traveler, please contact us for any inquiry"

• By car

Phuket is directly connected to the mainland by the Sarasin Bridge. From Bangkok, take Hwy 4 through Nakhon Pathom, Prachuap Khiri Khan, Chumphon, through Ranong province's Kra Buri and Kapoe districts, Phang Nga Province's Takua Pa and Thai Muang districts and onto Phuket Island. The total distance is 862 km. You may be better off getting to Phuket by public transport and renting a car on the island.

Getting In

● By boat

Ferry services connect from Rassada Port in Phuket Town to Ko Phi Phi and to Krabi Province on the mainland twice a day, taking 90 to 120 minutes. It's usually a pleasant ride, but can be rather bumpy when it's windy.

From the harbour, you could avoid the minibuses and take a songthaew to Phuket Town. If it doesn't show up at the bus stop right outside the terminal, you'll have to walk past the gate outside the harbour and along the road, turning left at the first T-junction, about 600 m, then on the main road you can catch a cheap songthaew. There's a picture of all the routes posted just outside the terminal near the bus stop inside the complex. Last one leaves at 19:00.

There are speedboats from/to Ko Racha (45 minutes), Phi Phi (1 - 1.5 hours), the Similan Islands (about 3 hours) and other islands. Boats and yachts can be chartered all year from Phuket at Chalong Bay, Rawai Beach, the Boot Lagoon, the Yacht Haven and Royal Phuket Marina. Boats from Phi Phi and Phang Nga can be found by visiting the local beaches. A search for Phuket speedboat charters will turn up many companies providing inter-island charters and services.

Getting In

● By boat

Phi Phi speedboat transfers (no tour) are provided by the Zeavola Resort, which has dedicated speedboats for Phi Phi transfers. Most companies doing Phi Phi speedboat tours will not accommodate transfers that include baggage due to space limitations.

Prices for speedboat charters to/from Phuket depend on distance/size of boat.

It's possible to visit Phuket by cruise ship. For cruises from Singapore, try Star Cruises (check it on Internet)

Getting Around

Phuket is a large island and you need some form of transport to get around. Public transport is very limited and taxis and tuk-tuks are the only practical means. Another, more dangerous option is rent your own wheels. Hotels generally offer shuttle bus services into Phuket Town, and also have taxi and car hire facilities.

● Songthaew

This is the cheapest public transport in Phuket. Represent extra-long pickups of various forms.Within Phuket Town buses run pink, and beyond, to other beaches and areas, go blue. Almost everyone has an inscription in English about the route.

Pink - fare 15 baht. The bus runs from 6:30 to 20:30.

The route number is indicated on the windshield on the left side

● Smart buses

In 2018, Phuket has a very convenient and comfortable bus-Phuket Smart bus.

Travel inexpensive from 50 to 170 baht. Thanks to him, you can not only get from the airport to the beach, but also cheap to move between the main beaches of the Western part of the island. Travel between neighboring costs 50 baht.

Getting Around

● Smart buses

On the first trip you need to buy a plastic ticket, which is called Phuket Rabbit card. It costs 300 baht, of which 100 baht is the cost of the card itself, which is not refundable, and the card account is only 200 baht. You can travel if the card amount is not less than 170 baht. The card validity period is 7 years

As of May 2022, the cost of the bus has been lowered to THB 100 / trip, regardless of where you board and depart.

● Tuk-tuk

The minimum fare is 200 baht. The cost of an hour of rent will be-200 baht. At the same time it can accommodate up to 4 - 8 people. At night, drivers throw an additional 50% of the cost

● Motorbike Taxi

The fare starts from 20 baht for 1-2 km, they are almost at every corner. Drivers are dressed in bright numbered vests

● Prepaid (taxi prepaid)

In any tour office both in the international and domestic terminal of Phuket airport you will be offered a taxi to the desired hotel / beach. You just pay the full amount of the trip, you are given a receipt, which indicates the number of the car, go to the Parking lot, look for a car with the specified number and go to the right place.

Getting Around

Smart buses

If you leave the airport building on the street, you will see a counter where you can take a taxi. Rates are as follows :

- ☑ 100 baht airport fee
- ☑ 50 baht-first two kilometers
- ☑ next 2-15 km-12 baht per km
- ☑ next 10 km-15 baht per km

Motorbike rental

Bike rental locations are located in almost every quarter. Standard rental price - from 150 baht (the cost of rent depends on the duration and model). When you rent you need a passport or a Deposit.

Car rental

Rent at the airport, as there is rent in the city. The longer the rental period, the lower the price per day. Standard rental price - from 600 baht (the cost of rent depends on the duration and model). Rent a car in Phuket is available for citizens who have reached the age of 20 years.

To rent a car you will need a passport and a photocopy of it, international law.

Must-See

Phuket is known the world over for its beaches. There is a wide variety of beaches, some calm, some totally ruined by millions of visitors each year. But you can explore the interior of Phuket, a fertile hilly expanse that consists of mangrove forests, fishing villages, rubber and pineapple plantations, small Muslim communities and shrimp farms.

Activities

Swimming, snorkelling, diving, yachting, sailing, jet-skiing and parasailing are among the more popular activities on the island. Other activities include freediving, windsurfing, kite surfing, wakeboarding, and deep sea fishing. Popular kite surfing locations include Nai Yang in summer and Chalong Bay in winter season. Sea canoeing is a popular activity in Phang Nga Bay, as many grottoes are only accessible by canoe. Sailing Regattas include the Kings Cup in December, Pangna Bay Regatta normally in February and Phuket Raceweek in July.

Activities

• Diving

Phuket has some decent dive sites. Most dive sites are off nearby islands, but distances are fairly short and there are dozens of dive shops and boats to cater to your needs, most based near Chalong Bay. The reefs in the area are in a healthy condition with both solid hard corals and colourful soft corals. There is also an abundance of marine life. Most of the dive locations are suitable for all levels of divers, but there are also some that are quite deep.

The most well-known dive site in the Phuket area is Racha Yai with its sloping rocky reefs and its abundance of solid coral forests. It is home to Ter Bay where there is an exciting wreck in the depths of 25–35 m. The island south of Racha Yai, Racha Noi, is a haven for experienced divers as the depths are greater and the currents stronger. The overall topography is strikingly different from Racha Yai with huge granite boulders. The diving in Racha Noi compared to Racha Yai is definitely more challenging but the rewards are greater.

Expressive Image

Activities

Freediving

Phuket is a leading dive centre in Thailand and has become a freediving hotspot. It is the home of the area's only AIDA instructor training centre. Most freediving trips go out with scuba dive boats to well-trafficked dive sites, but some freediving off the beach is also possible. The local operators are usually very happy to find like-minded divers and will happily give pointers.

Sailing and yachting

Phuket is a leading dive centre in Thailand and has become a freediving hotspot. It is the home of the area's only AIDA instructor training centre. Most freediving trips go out with scuba dive boats to well-trafficked dive sites, but some freediving off the beach is also possible. The local operators are usually very happy to find like-minded divers and will happily give pointers.

Snorkelling

Snorkelling can be enjoyed in sheltered bays all around Phuket. It is particularly enjoyable at easily accessible reefs at Patong, Karon and Kata Beaches. Fins, mask, and snorkel can be rented on a daily basis from shops all over the island. Full and half day trips are available to the islands surrounding Phuket.. Research your options before signing up for any tour.

Things to buy

Phuket Town is a source of cultured pearls, niello ware, pewter ware, ornaments and dried seafood. Specialist shops dealing in souvenir products can be found on Ratsada, Phang Nga, Montri, Yaowarat, and Tilok-U-Thit Rd, in Phuket Town, Thepkasattri Rd, north of town and at the beach centres of Patong, Kata, Karon, and Rawai. Phuket's larger beaches are ravaged by ravenous hordes of tailors, who are certainly cheap, but will screw you over if they can. For example, suits done in 24 hours are usually just glued together and will fall apart the first time you take them to a dry cleaner. Choose your own fabrics (you can buy them on Thalang Rd in Phuket Town), insist on multiple fittings and check the quality of work carefully. It makes little difference which tailor shop you choose, since they're all just sales fronts for a few central sweatshops.

There are two giant shopping malls in Phuket: Central Festival, at the northwest edge of Phuket Town, and Jungceylon, in Patong.

There is a night market that opens from Th-Su, a couple of traffic lights past the Central Festival shopping mall. You can buy many things from clothes to jewellery to sunglasses. A great place to visit during your stay.

Food

Food in Phuket is surprisingly cosmopolitan, especially in Patong, as many foreigners have set up shop to cater to their fellow travellers. All the usual Thai favourites are of course still available, with a particular emphasis on seafood. See the individual town articles for detailed listings. Phuket has its own style of preparation and cooking. Some interesting local dishes include:

Fried or boiled noodle dishes (หมี่ผัดหรือหมี่น้ำแบบต่าง ๆ), usually with pork or chicken, are available at many noodle shops in Phuket Town such as Mi Ton Pho, Mi Sapam, Mi Ao Ke, Mi Hun Pa Chang.

Khanom Jin (ขนมจีน), a version of noodles eaten at breakfast, usually served with a spicy curry sauce and fresh vegetables.

Nam Phrik Kung Siap (น้ำพริกกุ้งเสียบ) is a mixture of dried chili and smoked shrimp eaten with various fresh vegetables.

Cashew nuts and pineapples are grown in Phuket and available all year round. The nuts are available dried, fried, or coated. Phuket pineapples are some of the most delectable, sweet and firm available.

Sleep

There are lots of options available in Phuket. But for the more popular hotels and resorts in the better locations you should book at least a couple months in advance during high season (Nov-May). The best rates are usually found on-line and many hotels offer best rate guarantees when you book direct. Most of the time you will pay more if you walk in and take the rack-rate.

There are 5 main areas for tourists to stay in Phuket. Patong is the most popular due to its active nightlife, street markets and calm water beaches however this area isn't for everyone (especially people with families). The quieter areas include Kata, Karon, Rawai and Nai Yang, all with great markets and quieter beach areas.

Connect

Mail

If you want to send mail, post offices and parcel services are widely available. In Phuket Town, there is a post office at the corner of Phang Nga Rd and Montri Rd. In Patong, there is one at the appropriately named Soi Post Office, a side-street of Thavee Wong Rd (near Molly Malone's).

Telephone

You can usually pick up a free Thai SIM card at the airport in the baggage claim area. Look around for a booth or a kiosk.

The area code for Phuket is 076. Dial the 0 if you're calling from within Thailand.

Pay phones are uncommon, as most Thais have mobile phones. Phuket has very good mobile phone coverage. You can also pre-purchase a Thai SIM card online.

Mobile Internet is available from all providers. You can easily purchase a SIM and the Internet package at one of the numerous phone shops around Phuket.

Safety

Particularly in the summer monsoon season, there are strong currents on many of the beaches and drownings are a depressingly common occurrence. Four tourists died during a single 3-day stretch in Jun 2009. Heed the warning flags on popular beaches and play it safe if off the beaten track.

Crime as of late has definitely increased in the Phuket area among farangs (Westerners) and you should keep this in mind and be vigilant of anyone who wants to befriend you or trick you into gambling (which is illegal) or anything else you consider out of the ordinary. Katoeys (ladyboys) are notorious for pick-pocketing as you walk around the tourist areas at night. Also muggings do take place on a regular basis. Avoid walking down unlit sois; stick to the main roads. If something looks/sounds too good to be true, it surely is.

Tourist police can be contacted locally by dialing 1155. They have a good basic understanding of English (many are farangs), so if you're in trouble these people should be contacted first. Thai police speak hardly any English and normally take the side of the locals even if at fault. Always insist on the Tourist Police if you have any run-in with the Thai Police. Use only metered taxis and ask hotels to call, take down

Safety

driver license plate and taxi license number before you get in. You can use the receipt from a taxi to complain to police or find lost property, so take a receipt and license numbers. Don't overstay your visa! Two offices in Phuket can extend you visa. The extension is valid for extra 30 days of the leaving date stamped in your passport. The cost is 1900 baht. You'll need to provide a passport-sized photo. You can do it there. The Immigration Office in Phuket Town is at the end of Phuket Rd. close to the pier. There is another office in Patong.

Health

Tap water should be regarded as non-potable. Liquids from sealed bottles nearly always are, and should be used wherever possible, for example, when brushing your teeth. Restaurants universally purchase ice made from purified water.

- Hospitals :
• Bangkok Hospital Phuket (โรงพยาบาลกรุงเทพภูเก็ต), ☎ 1719, +66 76 354062.
• Phuket International Dental Center, ☎ +1 303 500 3821.
• Mission Hospital (โรงพยาบาลมิชชั่น), ☎ +66 76 23722026, fax: +66 76 211907. Emergency call 076 237227.

Safety

Health

• Patong-Kathu Hospital (โรงพยาบาลป่าตอง-กะทู้), ☎ +66 76 342633-4, fax: +66 76 340617. Emergency call 076 340444.

• Phuket International Hospital or Siriroj Hospital (โรงพยาบาลศิริโรจน์), ☎ +66 76 249400, fax: +66 76 210936.

• Thalang Hospital (โรงพยาบาลถลาง), ☎ +66 7 311111, +66 76 311033.

• Vachira Phuket Hospital (โรงพยาบาลวชิระภูเก็ต), ☎ 1669, +66 76 361234, fax: +66 76 211155.

Map

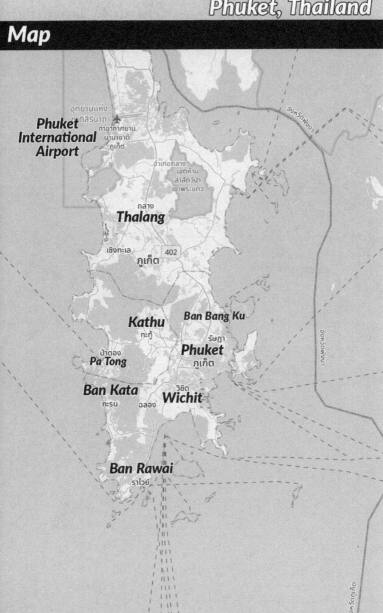

Photo Gallery

Phuket, Thailand

Photo Gallery

Photo Gallery

Phuket, Thailand

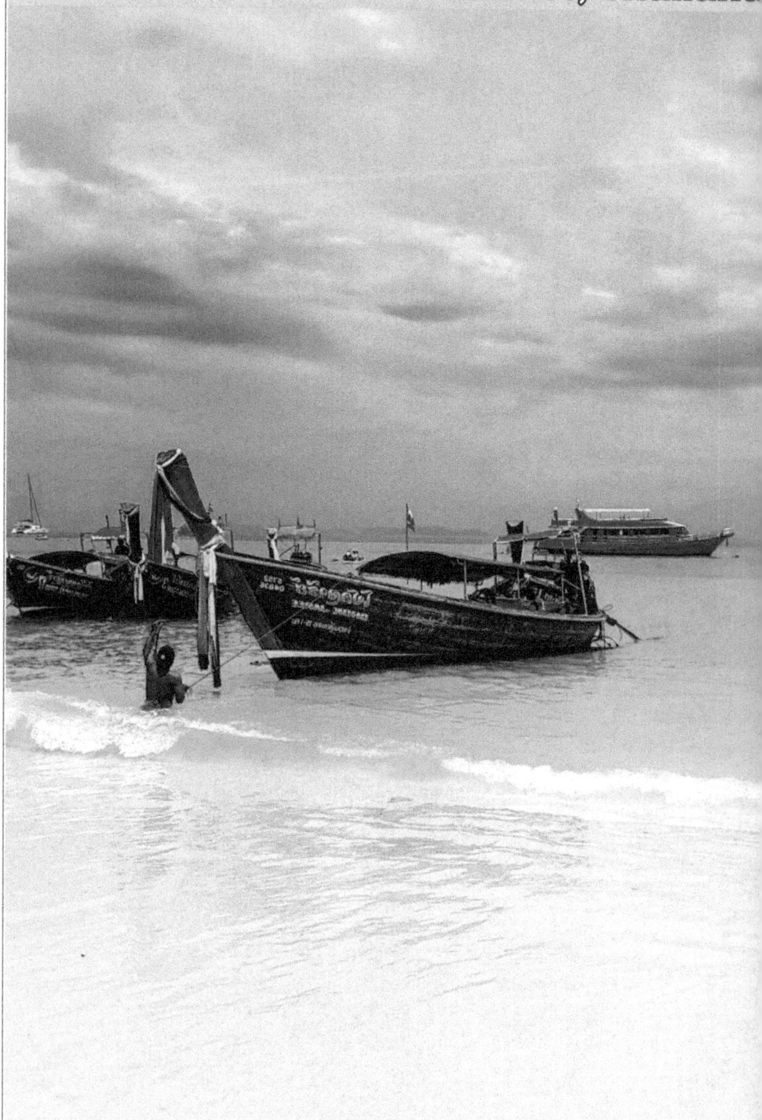

Photo Gallery

Photo Gallery

Krabi Province

Beach and water sports mecca in the south, includes Ao Nang, Rai Leh, Ko Phi Phi, and Ko Lanta

Krabi Province, Thailand

Overview

Krabi Province (จังหวัดกระบี่) is a popular beach destination on the Andaman Sea in Southern Thailand.

Cities

• Ao Nang — Krabi's most developed beach, a long beach fringed by palm trees

• Had Yao (Long Beach) — the last untouched beach in Krabi Province, and perhaps the most spectacular with its views of Jum Mountain and Ao Nang's cliff walls

• Krabi Town — the administrative capital and a common entry point into the region by boat or plane

• Rai Leh — one of Thailand's important rock climbing destinations, a craggy peninsula with several small beaches

• Ton Sai — cheapest bungalows in the area, preferred by backpackers away from the hordes of tourists and an easy walk to Rai Leh

Map

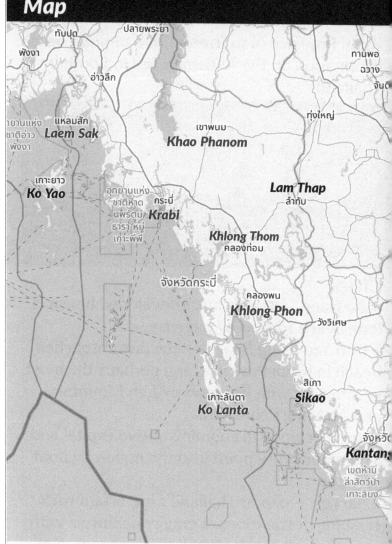

ทับปุด
ปลายพระยา
พังงา
ทานพอ
ฉวาง
อ่าวลึก
จันดี
ยานแห่ง
ชาติอ่าว
พังงา
แหลมสัก
Laem Sak
ทุ่งใหญ่
เขาพนม
Khao Phanom
เกาะยาว
Ko Yao
Lam Thap
ลำทับ
อุทยานแห่ง
ชาติหาด
นพรัตน์
ธารา-หมู่
เกาะพีพี
กระบี่
Krabi
Khlong Thom
คลองท่อม
จังหวัดกระบี่
คลองพน
Khlong Phon
วังวิเศษ
สิเภา
Sikao
เกาะลันตา
Ko Lanta
จังหวั
Kantang
เขตห้าม
ล่าสัตว์ป่า
เกาะลิบง
อุทยานแห่ง
ชาติหมู่เกา
เกตรา

 : **Belong to Krabi**

 : **Do not belong to Krabi**

Krabi Province, Thailand

Overview

Attractions

• Baan Ao Leuk - some caves here well worth a visit.

• Ko Hong - group of islands between Krabi and Ko Yao, with the main island being popular for kayaking due to its picturesque lagoon

2• Ko Jum — peace & quiet for those looking for solitude

• Ko Lanta — sleepy island, the new escape for those who find Ao Nang/Rai Leh too touristy

• Ko Ngai — part of Krabi Province, but easier to reach from Trang

• Ko Phi Phi — Thailand's largest marine national park where The Beach was filmed

• Ko Poda - known by tourists as "4 islands", it is an archipelago nearby Ao Nang and Rai Leh

• Ko Por — an eco-tourism place near the island of Ko Lanta

• Ko Siboya — rural Thailand with a difference

Krabi Province, Thailand

Map

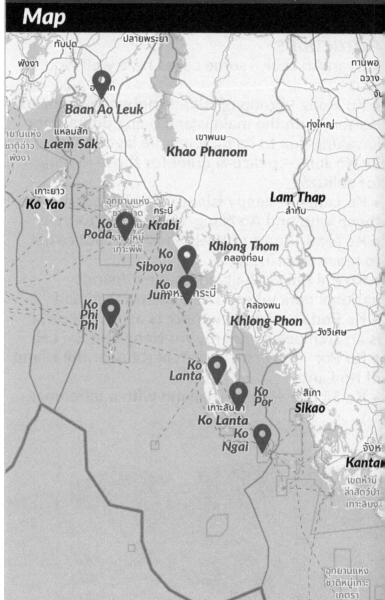

Krabi Province, Thailand

Learn more

Krabi, a coastal province, abounds with countless natural attractions that never fail to impress tourists. Such attractions include white sandy beaches, crystal clear water, fascinating coral reefs, caves and waterfalls, as well as numerous islands.

The distinguishing feature of both Krabi and neighboring Phang Nga is the massive limestone karsts, rising vertiginously out of the flat rice paddies on land and as islands from the sea. Add in some gorgeous beaches, excellent scuba diving, and rock climbing, and it's little wonder that tourism in the area has been booming.

While less commercialized than neighboring Phuket, Krabi Province cannot be described as undiscovered: it receives two million visitors a year, and the major tourist areas cater to foreigners. The upside of Krabi, when compared to Phuket, is that many of the most beautiful beaches can only be accessed by boat, such that their coastal villages are far less urbanised and more laid back, a relief for those who do not want to see McDonald's or Starbucks and open air prostitution. The downside is the massive traffic of boats to these beaches, especially in high season, affecting the environment and the tranquility, to the point that it sometimes may be hard to find a spot in the beach to swim.

Krabi Province, Thailand

Learn more

History

From archaeological discoveries, it is believed that Krabi was one of the oldest communities in Thailand dating back to the prehistoric period. It is believed that this town may have taken its name after the meaning of Krabi, which means "sword". This may have stemmed from a legend that an ancient sword was unearthed prior to the city's founding.

Krabi Province was badly hit by the Indian Ocean tsunami of December 2004. Signs of the damage are now hard to find.

Climate

The best time to visit Krabi is between the months Nov-Apr when the area's climate is cooler. During this period the island gets a lot of dry northeasterly winds, delivering blue skies and starry nights. Down on the beaches one can enjoy nice sea breezes. From Jun-Nov the area gets a lot of rainfall, more on average than the rest of the country. During this period the island gets a lot of moist southwesterly winds, resulting in a mix of dry and wet days. The sea stays at a warm 29°C all year round. Off-setting the less favourable weather, visitors during this period will find it cheaper.

Krabi Province, Thailand

Learn more

Geology

Bordering the Andaman Sea, Krabi is 814 km south of Bangkok and covers an area of 4,708 km^2. Its mountainous physical geography is broken by highlands and plains, covering more than 130 large and small islands, and abounding with mangrove forests. The Krabi River flows 5 km through the town and into the Andaman Sea at Tambon Pak Nam. There are also klongs (canals) such as Klong Pakasai, Klong Krabi Yai, and Klong Krabi Noi, which all originate from Krabi's highest mountain, Mount Phanom Bencha.

- North : borders Phang Nga and Surat Thani
South : borders Trang and the Andaman Sea
- East : borders Nakhon Si Thammarat
- West : borders Phang Nga and the Andaman Sea

Language

You can get around on English alone in the more visited areas, although a few words of Thai will come in handy off the beaten track and will be much appreciated everywhere. Dive shops are polyglot, speaking a number of other European languages.

Krabi Province, Thailand

Getting In

The most popular way to enter this province is via its capital, Krabi Town.

● *By plane*

Krabi International Airport (KBV IATA) is about 10 km from the city limits, 15 km from the city centre, 40 km from Ao Nang, and 23 km from Had Yao. Thai Airways operates daily direct flights to/from Bangkok, as does Air Asia from Bangkok and Kuala Lumpur. Bangkok Airway flies to Ko Samui nearly every day of the week. Destination Air Shuttle, Thailand's only seaplane service, also routinely flies in and out of Krabi (Ko Lanta) from Phuket and to the numerous outer islands.

● *By car*

Krabi is on Hwy 4. Shared songthaews from Ao Nang to Krabi are frequent and cost 60 baht. Originating in Bangkok, Hwy 4 links many of the province's districts. Other main routes include:
● Hwy 4035 to Plai Phraya District (Krabi) and Phra Saeng district (Surat Thani)
● Hwy 4034 links Ao Nang and Nopparat Beaches
● Hwy 4037 to Khao Phanom District (towards Surat Thani)
● Hwy 4038 links Klong Thom and Lam Thap Districts
● Hwy 4206 links Klong Thom to Ko Lanta

Krabi Province, Thailand

Getting In

- From Bangkok:
- Proceed along Hwy 4, passing Phetchaburi–Prachuap Khiri Khan–Chumphon–Ranong–Phang Nga to Krabi. The distance is 946 km.
- Travel along Hwy 4 to Hwy 41 at Chumphon via Lang Suan and Chaiya, Surat Thani. Proceed towards Wiang Sa, change to Hwy 4035 for Baan Ao Luek, and switch back to Hwy 4 again to Krabi. This route is 814 km.
- From Phuket:
- Proceed along Hwy 402 and 4. The distance is 176 km.

• By bus

Krabi Province's bus terminal is in Krabi town.
- Krabi Bus Terminal. In Krabi buses use the bus terminal at Talad Kao, about 5 km north of town centre. It is one of Thailand's better bus stations: it's clean, has bilingual signage, a good cafe, many local transport options (motorbike taxi, songthaew, taxi, minivan), and free Wi-Fi. (Since Jan 2016)
There are regular direct bus services between Bangkok's Southern Bus Terminal and Krabi (~500 baht), but probably the best option is to take a VIP bus, which for 250 baht more makes the 10 hour ride much more comfortable.

Krabi Province, Thailand

Getting In

● By bus

Buses from Bangkok's Southern Bus Terminal (Tel. ☎ +66 2 4351199) to Krabi take about 12 hours and depart as follows:

VIP bus - 07:20 - 1,055 baht
First class bus - 19:00 - 680 baht
Second class bus - 07:30, 19:00, 19:30, 21:00 - 37 baht

● By train

The nearest train stations are in Surat Thani and in Trang.

Surat Thani - 3-4 hours away from Krabi by bus.
Trang - 2-2.5 hours away from Krabi by bus.

Getting Around

● Songthaew*

Various tourist attractions can be conveniently reached by local songthaew. Destinations includ Ban Huai To, Ban Nong Thale, Ban Khao Thong, Hat Noppharat Thara, Susan Hoi, Ao Nang, Ban Khlong Muang, Ban Nai Sa, Khao Phanom, Nuea Khlong, Khlong Thom, Ban Bo Muang, Ban Hua Hin, Ban Khlong Phon, Lam Thap, Baan Ao Luek, and Plai Phraya. Songthaews depart from the Vogue Department Store on Maha Rat Rd. Trips other destinations can be made by taxi and renta car.

Songthaew* : It's a pickup car or a Tuk-tuk

Getting Around

● *Boating*

Krabi is mostly coast and islands, so you'll be spending quite some time on boats when getting around. The most common boat type for shorter hops is the longtail boat (reua hang yao), which true to its name has the propeller at the end of a long drive shaft stretching from the boat. This makes them supremely manoeuvrable even in shallow waters, but they're a little underpowered for longer trips and you'll get wet if it's even a little choppy.

Krabi Province, Thailand

Attractions

● Hat Noppharat Thara - Mu Ko Phi Phi National Park (อุทยานแห่งชาติหาดนพรัตน์ธารา – หมู่เกาะพีพี). Hat Noppharat Thara–Mu Ko Phi Phi National Park has an area of 242,437 rai (38,790 ha) of which 200,849 rai (32,136 ha) is sea. There are three distinctive kinds of forest here: moist evergreen forests, mangrove forests, and peat swamp forests. (Since Jan 2016)

● Mu Ko Phi Phi (หมู่เกาะพีพี) Forty-two kilometres from the provincial town of Krabi, Mu Ko Phi Phi (Phi Phi Islands) are an archipelago, formerly called Pulao Piah Pi. The surrounding sea is home to a variety of underwater anemones, coral reefs, and marine life. The area is a popular destination for snorkelling.

Attractions of Mu Ko Phi Phi :

● Ko Phi Phi Don Covers an area of 28 square km. Popular attractions are the twin bays with curving beaches of Ao Ton Sai and Ao Lo Da Lam.

● Ko Phi Phi Lee Occupying an area of only 6.6 square kilometres, Phi Phi Lee Island is surrounded by limestone mountains and sheer cliffs plunging hundreds of metres to the sea. The sea is 20 meters deep and the deepest point in the south of the island is around 34 meters. Ko Phi Phi Lee has bays such as Ao PiLe, and AoLo SaMa. In the northeast is a large cave called Tham Viking.

Krabi Province, Thailand

Attractions

- Su-san Hoi (Shell Cemetery) (สุสานหอย). Once a large freshwater swamp, the habitat of diverse mollusks of about 2 cm in size, Su-san Hoi features a slab formed from a huge number of embedded mollusks which can be dated to approximately 40 million years ago. With changes on the surface of the earth, seawater flooded the freshwater swamp and the limestone elements in the seawater enveloped the submerged mollusks resulting in a homogeneous layer of fossilized shells 40 cm thick known as Shelley limestone. With geographical upheavals, the limestone layer is now distributed in great broken sheets of impressive magnitude on the seashore. (Since Jan 2016)

- Ao Nang (อ่าวนาง) Ao Nang Beach is Krabi's most developed beach. Fringed by palms, the long beach is backed by a wide range of accommodation including resorts, bungalows, and guesthouses. A large selection of restaurants, and Western fast food chains can also be found here.

- Hat Rai Leh (Rai Leh Beach East/West) Hat Rai Leh is bounded on two sides by limestone cliffs, thus isolating it from the mainland. It is only accessible by boat. Rai Leh West has a white sand beach and is the longest of the beaches in this area.

Krabi Province, Thailand

Attractions

Rai Leh East is popular backpacker hang-out and offers cheaper accommodation than the west side. Rai Leh East's beach has extensive stands of mangroves, making it less suitable for beach activities.

• Pra Nang Beach (Princess Cave Beach) Adjacent to Rai Leh, has a good beach and is the site of a luxury resort.

• Than Bok Khorani National Park (อุทยานแห่งชาติธารโบกขรณี). he park covers an area of 121 km2. The landscape is dominated by a series of limestone mountains, evergreen forests, mangrove forests, and numerous islands. The main flora is evergreen forest, peat swamp forest, strand forest, and mangrove forest, as wel as various types of marine flora. Other attractions include: Than Bokkhorani which is home to various flowing streams and numerous pools of different cascades among a shady forested area and two caves, Tham Lot and Tham Phi Hua To. (Since 2016)

• Namtok Ron Khlong Thom (น้ำตกร้อนคลองท่อม). An area of hot springs in a shady forest. The temperature is at 40-50 degrees Celsius. The hot springs and cool streams converge on a slope to form cascades of warm water. (Since 2016)

Krabi Province, Thailand

Attractions

• Khao Pra–Bang Khram Wildlife Sanctuary (เขตรักษาพันธุ์สัตว์ป่าเขาประ–บางคราม) At Tambon Khlong Thom Nuea. Composed of lowland forest, this area features the Emerald Pool or Sa Morakot, which are three hot springs with a temperature of 30–50 degrees Celsius. The forest is home to varied flora and rare birds like Gurney's pitta, rufous-collared kingfisher, and black hornbill. There is a 2.7 km nature trail known as the Tina Jollife (Thung Tiao) Trail, named after an English conservationist.

• Mu Ko Lanta National Park (อุทยานแห่งชาติหมู่เกาะลันตา). Covering a total area of 152 km2, Mu Ko Lanta National Park is in Amphoe Ko Lanta and consists of many islands. Some major islands are Ko Lanta Yai, Ko Lanta Noi, Ko Taleng Beng, as well as, other surrounding islands like Mu Ko Ha, Mu Ko Rok, and Ko Ngai. (Since 2016)

• Pa Phru Tha Pom Khlong Song Nam Pa Phru or peat swamp forest of the canal of Tha Pom features a number of water sources, which originate from the Chong Phra Kaeo pool. Tha Pom is called "khlong song nam" by locals, which in Thai literally means "two water canal". Here, clear freshwater, in which the pool's floor and the roots of Lumphi the palm (Eleiodoxa conferta) are visible, meets seawater from the mangrove forest.

Food

Much of the cuisine has its origins in Malay, Indonesian, and Indian food. Favourite dishes from the south include Indian-style Muslim curr (massaman), rice noodles in fish curry sauce (khanom chin), and khao mok kai (chicken biryani). Unsurprisingly for a coastal region, seafood features prominently on the menu. Traditional southern Thai food includes milder coconut-milk based curries popularly associated with Thailand: the dry, Malaysian-influenced Panang curry and Indian-influenced massaman (Muslim) curry with potatoes and nuts.

The wing shell (หอยชักตีน) is Krabi's best-know dish. In addition, stir-fried spotted Babylon (หอยหวาน) with chilies and basil is also noteworthy.

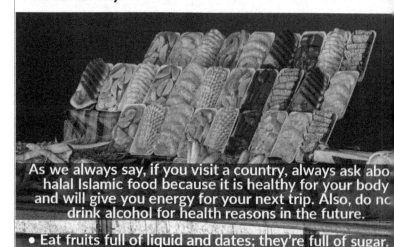

As we always say, if you visit a country, always ask abo halal Islamic food because it is healthy for your body and will give you energy for your next trip. Also, do nc drink alcohol for health reasons in the future.

• Eat fruits full of liquid and dates; they're full of sugar.

Krabi Province, Thailand

Food

Restaurants (In Krabi Town)

● Arun (Near Relax). Good breakfast place with decent Thai coffee. Closed during low season.

● Le Gateau (Utarakit Rd). 10:00-21:00. Charming little French place that serves good coffees and desserts, Thai food, and a limited Western menu featuring steaks. Good place to take a date. (Since Jan 2016)

● May & Mark's House Cafe & Restaurant, 6 Maharaj Soi 10, ☎ +66 75 612562, maymark2544@yahoo.com. 07:00-21:00. The story of this restaurant is fascinating. Husband and wife Matee and Kittiya opened a small restaurant in 1990. It was named May and Mark after their two children. It offered a selection of pre-cooked curries to be served over rice. Travelers would stop and stare at the pots of curry, then move on. The owners did not know why. Later they figured out that farangs were unaccustomed to eating food that had been cooked and then left to sit. To lure farangs, the owners added pancakes to the menu. Things didn't improve much. To make ends meet they started renting out rooms above the restaurant. One boarder, a man named John Kean from New Zealand, stayed for two months. When he was not off exploring Krabi, he taught the owners how to bake bread and prepare farang food.

Food

Restaurants (In Ao Nang)

• Isan Food & Cooking Inter (Central Ao Nang, road side opposite McDonalds, a few steps from Soi RCA, between currency exchange and Chanaya's Restaurant). Evenings. Weird name for a restaurant, but it doesn't matter as there is only one sign on the back wall of the restaurant's interior. Run by a lady (Noi?) from Issan. One of the cheapest restaurants in central Ao Nang. Simple Issan cooking. Large fish (tilapia?) seem to be the most popular fare here. Good and cheap. (Since Apr 2016)

• Carnivore, 127 Moo 3, ☎ +66 75 661 061, info@carnivore-thailand.com. Daily, 15:00-23:00; kitchen open 16:00-22:00. Known for delicious steaks, beef or lamb. Chicken, pork, and duck as well, all prepared to high European standards. Luckily, you can order the steak in a size to suit your appetite or your budget: 200-400 grams. Nice ambience. The boss, Gidi, is a friendly Dutch national who runs a tight ship to high standards. Huge wine and European beer lists. (Since Feb 2016)

"For any questions, please try to contact us; we are at your service!"

Sleep

Hotels *(In Ao Nang)*

• J Hotel, 23/3 Moo 2 (Up a small soi on the inland side of the road just south of the Irish Rover Pub sign), ☎ +66 75 637878, j_hotel@hotmail.com. This small hotel beats PK Mansion hands down. Chinese-Thai-run hotel. Impeccably clean. Big rooms, big baths. Rooms in back have balcony that face a wall, thus are much cheaper than those in front which overlook a parking area. Free, strong Wi-Fi. Nearby is its sister hotel, J Mansion. 800+ baht (500 baht in Sept. 18).

• Krabi Riviera Villas (Krabi Villas), 251/13 Moo 2, ☎ +66 75 695633, info@krabivilla.com. 17 villas for rent nightly/weekly with private swimming pool on Ao Nang Beach. 5,000-19,000+ baht.

Hotels *(In Krabi Town)*

• A Mansion Hotel, 12/6 Chao Fa Rd (near Tamarind Restaurant). A modern place with free high-speed Wi-Fi that reaches most of the rooms. 450-840 baht.

• Phanom Bencha Mountain Resort, ☎ +66 75 660501, info.pbmr@gmail.com. This garden resort is a 50-minute ride from downtown Krabi and the airport, and has a natural swimming pool and trekking opportunities in the adjacent Phanom Bencha National Park. This is an eco-resort. Low/high season prices are: double bungalows for 4 people 1,200/1,500 baht; single bungalows 600/900 baht.

Krabi Province, Thailand

Map (Krabi Town) (Restaurants Section) (Hotels Section)

Note : For more recommendations, please contact us, and we will serve you as much as possible.

ถนนศรีพังงา 4

58 m

ถนนอุตรกิจ

ถนนมหาราช

ถนนภาจรัส

ถนนกระบี่

Le Gateau

May & Mark's House
Cafe & Restaurant

Arun

A Mansion
Hotel

Baan Ao Leuk
Laem Sak

Ko Yao

Khao Phanom

Lan Thap

Khlong Thom

Krabi

Ko
PN
Phi

Ko
Jum

Khlong Phon

Ko
Lanta

Ko
Por

Ko
Siloso

Ko Lanta
Ko
Nga

Kantang

Krabi Town

Map (Ao Nang) (Restaurants Section) (Hotels Section)

Photo Gallery

Krabi Province, Thailand

Photo Gallery

Photo Gallery

Photo Gallery

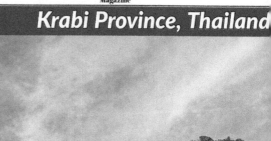

Photo Gallery

Photo Gallery

Date : . . / . . / . .

Have a great time in Thailand!

Date : . . / . . / . .

Have a great time in Thailand!

Date : . . / . . / . .

Have a great time in Thailand!

Help us grow!

Since we just started, and because we have worked so hard to make this book suitable for all classes of readers, feel free to leave a review on the purchase page!

★ ★ ★ ★ ☆

Jobs / Marketing

Because the brand is newly-established. If you are a fan of traveling around the world, you can join us for free, share your talent, and maybe we can hire you!

E-book Request

Please send the code below to get your free e-book via e-mail :
elghalia.help@outlook.com  DMTHAILAND_2023

Read it

We're trying to give the suitable information to the reader, and we work day by day to optimize our books. We apologize for any unintentional mistakes, but we always strive forward.

Travel safe!

EL GHALIA
Magazine

Made in the USA
Las Vegas, NV
29 April 2023